Azure Fundamentals

Develop and Deploy Cloud Solutions with Confidence

THOMPSON CARTER

Table of Content

TABLE OF CONTENTS

INTRODUCTION

WHY THIS BOOK MATTERS

Cloud computing is no longer a futuristic concept—it's **the present and the future** of technology. **Microsoft Azure** stands at the forefront of this cloud revolution, empowering individuals and businesses to **build, deploy, and scale applications faster than ever before**.

But if you've ever tried to learn cloud computing, you might have felt **overwhelmed** by **technical jargon, complex documentation, and endless service options. That's where this book comes in.**

"Azure Fundamentals: Develop and Deploy Cloud Solutions with Confidence" is designed to be your **step-by-step guide** to **understanding and mastering Azure**— whether you're an absolute beginner, a software developer, an IT professional, or a business leader looking to leverage the cloud.

This book will take you from the **foundations of cloud computing** to **real-world deployments**, ensuring that you not only understand **how Azure works** but also how to **apply it to practical, industry-relevant scenarios**.

Why Learn Azure?

Microsoft Azure is one of the **top cloud platforms in the world**, powering businesses, governments, and startups across **healthcare, finance, retail, and artificial intelligence (AI)**.

Azure's Growing Dominance

✓ **Over 95% of Fortune 500 companies** use Azure for cloud   solutions.
✓ **A leader in hybrid cloud, AI, and security**, according to Gartner.
✓ **High demand for Azure professionals**, with millions of cloud-related job openings globally.

Cloud computing is not **just for engineers**—businesses, project managers, analysts, and security professionals **all need cloud knowledge**.

By learning Azure, you are **future-proofing your career** and opening doors to exciting **cloud-related job opportunities** in **DevOps, security, data analytics, machine learning, and enterprise architecture.**

Who Is This Book For?

This book is for **anyone** looking to develop **a strong foundation in Microsoft Azure.** Whether you are:

✅ **A beginner** who wants to understand cloud computing from the ground up.

✅ **An IT professional** transitioning to cloud technologies.

✅ **A developer** looking to deploy and scale applications in the cloud.

✅ **A DevOps engineer** automating deployments with Azure.

✅ **A security professional** managing cloud compliance and governance.

✅ **A business leader** exploring cloud solutions for enterprise scalability.

We **break down complex concepts** into **easy-to-understand, jargon-free explanations** so that **anyone**—regardless of background—can grasp Azure **with confidence**.

What You'll Learn in This Book

This book is **structured into five parts**, guiding you from **Azure basics** to **advanced cloud deployments**.

📌 Part I: Understanding Cloud and Azure Basics

- **What is cloud computing?** Why businesses are moving to the cloud.
- **How Azure works** and how it compares to AWS and Google Cloud.
- **Setting up your first Azure account** and navigating the Azure Portal.
- **Core Azure services**, including computing, storage, networking, and security.

📌 Part II: Developing Cloud Solutions with Azure

- How to **deploy virtual machines, databases, and cloud storage**.

- **Azure networking fundamentals** to connect services securely.
- **Security best practices**, including **Azure Active Directory and compliance standards**.
- **Monitoring and logging** to track application health and performance.

★ Part III: Building and Deploying Solutions on Azure

- **Azure DevOps** and how to automate software deployments.
- **Serverless computing** with **Azure Functions** for event-driven applications.
- **Deploying containerized applications** using **Azure Kubernetes Service (AKS)**.
- **Scaling applications** with **Azure Load Balancers and Auto-Scaling**.

★ Part IV: Governance, Integration, and Advanced Deployment

- **Hybrid cloud solutions** integrating on-premises with Azure.
- **Using third-party tools** like **GitHub, Salesforce, and AWS** with Azure.

- **Advanced CI/CD pipelines** for enterprise deployments.
- **Security governance** to **meet compliance in regulated industries.**

📌 Part V: The Future of Azure and Cloud Computing

- **Emerging trends** like **edge computing, AI, and sustainability.**
- **How Azure is shaping the future of digital transformation.**
- **Career opportunities in Azure** and how to get certified.
- **Inspiring real-world case studies** of businesses using Azure to drive innovation.

What Makes This Book Different?

There are plenty of books on Azure, but **this one stands out because:**

✓ **Jargon-Free Approach** – We avoid unnecessary complexity and explain everything in **plain English.**
✓ **Real-World Applications** – Every chapter includes **practical, industry-relevant examples.**
✓ **Step-by-Step Learning** – No prior cloud experience

needed—we **start with the basics and build up gradually.**

✓ **Hands-On Exercises** – Learn by doing! We provide **real-life deployment examples** you can try on your own.

✓ **Future-Focused Insights** – We cover not just **Azure today,** but **where cloud computing is heading.**

By the end of this book, you'll not only **understand how Azure works**—you'll know **how to use it in real-world scenarios.**

Why Now is the Best Time to Learn Azure

The world is becoming **more cloud-dependent every day,** and businesses are looking for **cloud professionals** to help them **migrate, secure, and scale** their operations.

With Azure skills, you can:

✓ **Accelerate your career** with **high-paying cloud job opportunities.**

✓ **Help businesses innovate** using **cloud AI, IoT, and automation.**

✓ **Build scalable, high-performance applications** for the future.

✅ **Stay ahead of industry trends** as cloud computing continues to evolve.

There's never been a **better time** to dive into Azure. **Are you ready?** 🚀

How to Use This Book

You don't need to read this book cover to cover! Feel free to **jump to sections** that interest you the most.

💡 **If you're a beginner** → Start with **Part I: Azure Basics**.

💡 **If you're a developer** → Jump to **Part III: Building and Deploying Solutions**.

💡 **If you're focused on security and compliance** → Read **Part IV: Governance & Security**.

💡 **If you want to explore cutting-edge trends** → Check out **Part V: The Future of Azure**.

Final Words: Your Azure Journey Starts Now

Whether you're an **aspiring cloud professional**, a **developer**, or an **enterprise IT leader, Azure knowledge is one of the most valuable tech skills you can have today.**

This book will give you the confidence and practical skills to:

✓ **Build and deploy real-world cloud applications.**

✓ **Automate and optimize cloud operations.**

✓ **Secure cloud environments and meet compliance requirements.**

✓ **Innovate with AI, machine learning, and edge computing.**

Your **journey to mastering Azure** starts here. **Let's build the future together!** 🚀

Part I
Understanding Cloud and Azure Basics

CHAPTER 1

Introduction to Cloud Computing

Introduction

In today's fast-paced digital world, businesses of all sizes are embracing new ways to innovate and stay competitive. One of the most transformative shifts in recent decades is the move from traditional, on-premises IT infrastructures to cloud computing. This chapter introduces the concept of cloud computing, explores its evolution, and highlights its benefits over conventional methods. By the end of this chapter, you'll understand not only what cloud computing is but also why it has become a game changer for businesses—from startups to large enterprises.

What Is Cloud Computing?

Cloud computing is a way of delivering computing services—such as storage, processing power, and software—over the internet rather than using local servers or personal devices. In simpler terms, it means renting computing power from remote data centers, which are maintained and managed by cloud service providers.

Key Points:

- **On-Demand Access:** Cloud computing allows users to access applications and resources as needed, without having to invest in physical hardware.
- **Scalability:** It's easy to scale resources up or down based on current demand. Need more storage or processing power during peak times? Simply request more capacity.
- **Pay-As-You-Go Pricing:** Instead of purchasing expensive hardware that may be underutilized, cloud services typically charge based on actual usage. This model can lead to significant cost savings.

Imagine being able to run your business applications without worrying about maintaining servers or handling complex hardware setups. Instead, you focus on your business, while a trusted provider takes care of the computing infrastructure.

Advantages Over Traditional On-Premises Solutions

Traditional on-premises IT setups involve purchasing and managing your own hardware, software, and networks.

While this approach worked well in the past, it comes with several challenges compared to cloud computing.

1. Scalability

- **On-Premises:** Scaling up requires purchasing and installing additional hardware, which can be time-consuming and expensive.
- **Cloud:** Resources can be scaled instantly. Need more capacity? The cloud provider adds it for you with a few clicks or even automatically, based on your settings.

2. Flexibility

- **On-Premises:** Infrastructure is fixed and often tailored to a specific need, making it less adaptable to changing business requirements.
- **Cloud:** Offers the flexibility to experiment with new technologies and rapidly deploy or update applications without significant upfront investments.

3. Cost Efficiency

- **On-Premises:** Upfront capital expenditure for hardware, plus ongoing costs for maintenance, power, cooling, and staffing.

- **Cloud:** Reduced capital expenditure because you pay only for what you use. Additionally, cloud providers often offer cost management tools to help optimize spending.

4. Reliability and High Availability

- **On-Premises:** Achieving high availability can be challenging, requiring redundant hardware and complex configurations.
- **Cloud:** Providers operate multiple data centers around the globe. They ensure that your applications remain available even if one server or data center experiences an outage.

5. Focus on Innovation

- **On-Premises:** Significant resources and time must be dedicated to managing and maintaining infrastructure.
- **Cloud:** With infrastructure management offloaded to cloud providers, businesses can concentrate on developing new products and services, driving innovation.

The journey to cloud computing is one of continuous evolution. Let's take a brief look at how IT infrastructure has evolved over time.

Physical Servers

In the early days of computing, each application or service typically ran on its own physical server. This meant that organizations had to purchase and maintain a large number of servers, often resulting in underutilized resources and high operational costs.

Virtual Machines (VMs)

To improve resource utilization, virtualization emerged as a way to run multiple operating systems on a single physical server. Virtual machines allowed companies to consolidate workloads and make better use of their hardware. However, VMs still required a full operating system for each instance, which meant that there was significant overhead and less flexibility in scaling.

The Rise of Cloud Computing

Cloud computing built on the concepts of virtualization but took them further by abstracting the underlying hardware entirely. Instead of managing physical or virtual machines, businesses now access resources as a service. This shift has made it possible to deploy applications faster, scale seamlessly, and reduce costs dramatically.

Cloud computing is not just an evolution in technology—it represents a fundamental change in how IT services are delivered and consumed. By moving away from hardware-centric models, organizations are now empowered to innovate more rapidly and respond dynamically to market demands.

Real-World Example: A Small Business's Transition to the Cloud

Imagine a small local retail business that has been running its IT operations using a few on-premises servers. The company's servers host everything from their website and inventory management system to their customer relationship management (CRM) software. Over time, the business begins to experience several challenges:

- **High Maintenance Costs:** The company struggles with the expenses associated with purchasing new hardware, maintaining existing servers, and dealing with power and cooling costs.
- **Limited Scalability:** During peak sales seasons, the on-premises infrastructure cannot handle the increased traffic, leading to slow website performance and frustrated customers.
- **Operational Inefficiencies:** The IT team spends a significant amount of time troubleshooting hardware issues rather than focusing on improving business processes.

Recognizing these challenges, the business decides to move its IT infrastructure to the cloud. They choose a cloud service provider that offers a suite of services, including virtual machines, managed databases, and scalable storage.

The Transition Process

1. **Assessment   and   Planning:** The business conducts a thorough assessment of its current IT needs and future growth projections. They

plan the migration process, identifying which applications can be moved directly and which might need refactoring.

2. **Migration to the Cloud:** The company begins by migrating non-critical systems first, using cloud-based virtual machines to host their applications. Over time, they transition critical systems—like their e-commerce website and CRM—to managed services in the cloud.

3. **Benefits Realized:**

    o **Cost Savings:** The business experiences lower operational costs, as the pay-as-you-go pricing model reduces the need for large capital expenditures.

    o **Improved Performance:** The cloud's scalability ensures that during busy periods, additional resources are allocated automatically, keeping the website fast and responsive.

    o **Enhanced Focus:** With the cloud provider handling infrastructure management, the IT team can focus on improving business processes and developing new features.

This example illustrates how cloud computing can transform a business by reducing costs, increasing agility, and allowing the organization to focus on innovation rather than maintenance.

Conclusion

Cloud computing represents a significant shift from traditional on-premises infrastructure, offering numerous benefits that drive innovation, scalability, and cost efficiency. By understanding the basics of cloud computing—what it is, how it evolved, and why it's beneficial—you lay the foundation for exploring more advanced cloud solutions, especially those provided by Microsoft Azure.

Whether you're a small business owner, a developer, or an IT professional, this chapter has introduced you to the fundamental concepts that make cloud computing a vital tool for modern enterprises. As we move further into the book, you'll discover how these principles are applied within the Azure ecosystem, empowering you to develop and deploy cloud solutions with confidence.

Key Takeaways

1. **Cloud Computing Defined:**
   - o It is the delivery of computing services over the internet, allowing on-demand access to resources.

2. **Advantages Over On-Premises:**
   - o Cloud computing offers scalability, flexibility, cost efficiency, high availability, and the ability to focus on innovation.

3. **Evolution from Physical Servers to Cloud:**
   - o The progression from physical servers to virtual machines, and finally to the cloud, has enabled more efficient and agile IT operations.

4. **Real-World Impact:**
   - o A small business's transition from on-premises servers to the cloud can lead to reduced costs, improved performance, and greater operational agility.

Welcome to the journey of cloud transformation—let's explore how Azure can further empower you to develop and deploy cloud solutions with confidence!

CHAPTER 2

Overview of Microsoft Azure

Introduction

Microsoft Azure is one of the leading cloud platforms in the world, providing a vast array of services that help businesses deploy and manage applications with speed, agility, and confidence. In this chapter, we'll introduce you to Azure in an accessible, jargon-free way. You'll learn what Azure is, how its global infrastructure supports a wide range of cloud services, and why it has become an essential tool for organizations looking to modernize their IT operations. We'll also explore Azure's core offerings—including compute, storage, networking, and databases—and show you how Azure fits into today's cloud landscape through a real-world example of a retail chain using Azure to power its online store and manage customer data.

What is Microsoft Azure?

Microsoft Azure is a comprehensive cloud computing platform that offers an ever-expanding set of cloud services to build, deploy, and manage applications through Microsoft-managed data centers. Whether you are looking to host a simple website, build a complex machine learning application, or migrate entire data centers to the cloud, Azure provides the tools and services you need.

Key Points

- **On-Demand Services:** Azure allows you to use computing, storage, and networking resources on demand without the need to purchase or manage physical hardware.
- **Global Reach:** Azure is built on a global network of data centers, meaning you can deploy your applications close to your users around the world, reducing latency and improving performance.
- **Flexible Pricing:** With a pay-as-you-go pricing model, Azure helps you optimize costs by only charging for the resources you actually use.

- **Innovation   Platform:**
  Beyond basic infrastructure, Azure provides advanced tools for artificial intelligence, IoT, analytics, and DevOps, helping businesses innovate and stay competitive.

Azure's Global Infrastructure

One of the major strengths of Azure is its extensive global infrastructure. Azure is designed to offer high performance, scalability, and resilience by distributing services across multiple regions and Availability Zones.

Regions and Data Centers

- **Regions:**
  Azure is organized into regions, which are geographical areas that contain one or more data centers. This global network of regions ensures that your applications can be hosted close to your customers, improving speed and reliability.
- **Availability   Zones:**
  Within many Azure regions, data centers are further divided into Availability Zones. These zones are

physically separate locations within a region that protect your applications and data from localized failures, ensuring high availability and disaster recovery.

Benefits of a Global Infrastructure

- **Low   Latency:** By hosting applications in a region near your customers, Azure minimizes latency, providing a faster and smoother user experience.

- **Redundancy   and   Resilience:** With multiple regions and Availability Zones, Azure ensures that your applications remain online even if one data center experiences issues.

- **Regulatory   Compliance:** Azure's global footprint also helps businesses meet data residency and regulatory compliance requirements by allowing them to choose where their data is stored.

Core Azure Services

Azure offers a wide range of services designed to support every aspect of modern cloud computing. Below, we provide an overview of some of the key services in Azure that form the backbone of many cloud solutions.

Compute Services

Azure's compute services allow you to run applications in the cloud without worrying about underlying hardware.

- **Virtual Machines (VMs):** Deploy scalable and customizable Windows or Linux virtual machines to run applications, databases, or other workloads.

- **Azure App Service:** A fully managed platform for building, deploying, and scaling web applications and APIs. It handles infrastructure management so you can focus on coding.

- **Azure Functions:** A serverless compute service that enables you to run code on-demand without provisioning or managing servers. This is perfect for event-driven tasks.

- **Azure Kubernetes Service (AKS):** A managed container orchestration service that simplifies deploying and managing containerized applications using Kubernetes.

Storage Services

Azure offers various storage options to meet different needs—whether it's for files, structured data, or large amounts of unstructured data.

- **Azure Blob Storage:** Store massive amounts of unstructured data such as text or binary data, ideal for storing images, videos, and backups.
- **Azure File Storage:** Provides fully managed file shares that you can access via the standard SMB protocol.
- **Disk Storage:** Persistent, high-performance storage for Azure Virtual Machines.
- **Azure Data Lake Storage:** Designed for big data analytics workloads, offering scalable and secure data storage.

Networking Services

Networking in Azure connects your cloud resources securely and efficiently.

- **Virtual Networks (VNets):** Create isolated, private networks within Azure to securely connect your resources.
- **VPN Gateway:** Establish secure, cross-premises connectivity between your on-premises networks and Azure VNets.
- **ExpressRoute:** Provides a dedicated private connection between your on-premises infrastructure and Azure, offering more reliability and lower latencies compared to typical internet connections.
- **Load Balancer:** Distributes incoming traffic across multiple VMs or services, ensuring high availability and performance.

Database Services

Azure provides a variety of database solutions that cater to different application requirements.

- **Azure SQL Database:**
A fully managed relational database service built on SQL Server technology, optimized for modern cloud applications.

- **Azure Cosmos DB:**
A globally distributed, multi-model database service that provides low latency and high availability for mission-critical applications.

- **Azure Database for MySQL and PostgreSQL:**
Managed database services that offer enterprise-grade performance, scalability, and security for open-source databases.

- **Azure Cache for Redis:**
A fully managed in-memory data store that improves application performance by caching frequently accessed data.

Other Key Services

Azure is much more than just compute, storage, networking, and databases. It also offers a wide range of other services:

- **AI and Machine Learning:**
Tools such as Azure Machine Learning and

Cognitive Services help you build and deploy intelligent applications.

- **Internet of Things (IoT):** Services like Azure IoT Hub and IoT Central enable you to connect, monitor, and manage IoT devices at scale.

- **DevOps:**
Azure DevOps and Azure Pipelines streamline your development and continuous delivery processes.

- **Security and Compliance:** Azure Security Center and Azure Active Directory help you protect your resources and manage user access.

How Azure Fits into Today's Cloud Landscape

Azure has established itself as one of the top cloud platforms by offering a comprehensive set of services that address virtually every aspect of IT infrastructure and application development. Here's how Azure stands out in the cloud ecosystem:

- **Versatility:**
With offerings ranging from basic virtual machines

to advanced AI services, Azure can support small startups to large multinational enterprises.

- **Integration:**
Azure integrates seamlessly with other Microsoft products (such as Office 365 and Dynamics 365) and supports a wide range of third-party solutions, making it a flexible choice for organizations with diverse technology stacks.

- **Enterprise-Grade   Security:**
Built with strong security and compliance frameworks, Azure is trusted by businesses in highly regulated industries like finance and healthcare.

- **Global   Reach   and   Reliability:**
Its extensive global infrastructure ensures that applications can be deployed close to users and remain highly available even in the face of localized disruptions.

- **Innovation   and   Future-Readiness:**
Azure continues to evolve with emerging trends like serverless computing, edge computing, and artificial intelligence, ensuring that your organization can stay at the forefront of technology.

Real-World Example: A Retail Chain's Transformation with Azure

Consider a retail chain that operates hundreds of physical stores and a growing online presence. Historically, this chain managed its IT infrastructure with on-premises servers, hosting its website, inventory management system, and customer databases in-house. Over time, several challenges emerged:

- **Scalability** **Issues:** During peak shopping seasons, the online store experienced slowdowns and outages due to limited server capacity.

- **High** **Operational** **Costs:** Maintaining and upgrading physical servers was expensive and required constant manual intervention.

- **Limited** **Agility:** Rolling out new features or updates was slow, impacting the chain's ability to respond quickly to market trends and customer needs.

The Transition to Azure

To address these issues, the retail chain decided to migrate its IT infrastructure to Microsoft Azure. Here's how Azure made a difference:

1. **Scalability and Flexibility:** By moving to Azure, the chain leveraged virtual machines and Azure App Services to host its online store. During peak traffic periods, Azure's auto-scaling features automatically increased capacity, ensuring that the website remained responsive and fast.

2. **Cost Efficiency:** With Azure's pay-as-you-go model, the retail chain only paid for the resources it used. This eliminated the need for large upfront capital expenditures on hardware and reduced ongoing maintenance costs.

3. **Enhanced Data Management:** Azure's database services, such as Azure SQL Database and Cosmos DB, provided a secure and scalable platform for managing customer data and inventory information. This not only improved data reliability but also supported advanced analytics to drive better business decisions.

4. **Global Reach:** By deploying services across multiple Azure regions,

the chain ensured that its online presence was robust and highly available, even if one data center experienced issues. This geographic distribution also helped reduce latency, offering a smoother shopping experience for customers regardless of their location.

5. **Operational   Agility:**
With the cloud platform handling the heavy lifting of infrastructure management, the IT team was free to focus on innovation. New features and updates were rolled out faster, enabling the retail chain to stay competitive in a rapidly evolving market.

The Impact

After migrating to Azure, the retail chain saw a dramatic improvement in both performance and cost efficiency. The online store became more resilient during high-traffic events, operational costs dropped significantly, and the business gained the agility to innovate quickly. This transformation not only enhanced the customer experience but also provided a solid foundation for future growth.

Conclusion

Microsoft Azure is a powerful and versatile cloud platform that has redefined how businesses manage and deploy IT solutions. By providing a global infrastructure, a comprehensive suite of services, and the flexibility to scale on demand, Azure empowers organizations to overcome the limitations of traditional on-premises systems. Whether you're just starting your cloud journey or looking to modernize your existing infrastructure, understanding the core offerings of Azure is the first step toward developing and deploying cloud solutions with confidence.

In this chapter, we've explored what cloud computing is, the benefits it offers over traditional systems, and the evolution that led to the emergence of platforms like Azure. We've also taken a detailed look at Azure's global infrastructure and core services, concluding with a real-world example that demonstrates how a retail chain successfully transformed its operations by migrating to Azure.

As you continue reading, you'll delve deeper into Azure's capabilities and discover how to leverage these tools to build robust, scalable, and secure cloud solutions. Welcome to the world of Azure!

Key Takeaways

1. **Definition of Cloud Computing:**
   - o Cloud computing delivers on-demand computing resources over the internet, eliminating the need for physical hardware.

2. **Benefits Over Traditional Infrastructure:**
   - o Scalability, flexibility, cost efficiency, and high availability are among the top advantages of cloud computing.

3. **Evolution of IT Infrastructure:**
   - o The progression from physical servers to virtual machines and ultimately to cloud computing has paved the way for modern IT practices.

4. **Global Infrastructure of Azure:**
   - o Azure's global network of regions and Availability Zones ensures low latency, resilience, and compliance with data residency requirements.

5. **Real-World Impact:**
   - o A retail chain's migration to Azure demonstrates how cloud computing can transform business operations, reduce costs, and improve agility.

CHAPTER 3

Setting Up Your Azure Account and Navigating the Portal

Introduction

Before you can harness the power of Microsoft Azure, you need to create an account and become familiar with the Azure Portal—the central hub where you manage all your cloud resources. In this chapter, we will walk you through the process of signing up for Azure, setting up a subscription, managing billing, and navigating the intuitive interface of the Azure Portal. Whether you're a first-time cloud user or someone looking to streamline their cloud management, this chapter provides a clear, step-by-step guide to getting started with Azure.

Signing Up for Azure

Creating Your Azure Account

Azure offers a user-friendly sign-up process that opens the door to a comprehensive suite of cloud services. Here's what you need to know:

1. **Visit the Azure Website:**
   o Open your web browser and go to azure.microsoft.com.
   o Look for the "Start free" or "Free account" button to begin the registration process.

2. **Provide Your Information:**
   o You will be prompted to enter basic information such as your name, email address, and country.
   o Microsoft may ask for a phone number for identity verification. This step ensures that the account is secure and tied to a real user.

3. **Set Up Your Payment Method:**
   o Although Azure offers a free tier with credits to get you started, you will still need to provide a credit card or another payment method.
   o This payment information is used for billing once your free credits are exhausted. Azure's pricing is transparent, and you only pay for what you use.

4. **Confirm Your Subscription:**
   o Once your information is verified and your payment method is set up, your Azure account is

created, and you will be directed to the Azure Portal.

Managing Billing and Subscriptions

- **Subscription Overview:**
  - o In the Azure Portal, you can view all your subscriptions under the "Cost Management + Billing" section.
  - o A subscription represents a billing entity that groups your resources together. This is useful for tracking costs, applying budgets, and managing resources across different projects or departments.
- **Budgeting and Alerts:**
  - o Set up budgets and alerts within the billing dashboard to monitor your spending. Azure allows you to define spending thresholds, so you receive notifications if your costs approach or exceed your budget.
- **Usage Insights:**
  - o Explore detailed reports and dashboards that show your resource consumption. This transparency helps you optimize your spending by understanding which services are most cost-effective.

Once your account is set up, the Azure Portal is your control center. Let's explore the key elements of the portal:

The Dashboard

- **Customizable Interface:**
  - o The dashboard is your home screen when you log in to the Azure Portal. You can customize it to show the resources and metrics most important to you.
  - o Add tiles that display your recent activity, cost data, or performance metrics.

Menus and Navigation

- **Global Navigation Bar:**
  - o At the top of the portal, the global navigation bar provides quick access to the most used services such as "All services," "Cost Management + Billing," "Resource groups," and more.
- **Search Functionality:**
  - o The search bar lets you quickly find specific services, resources, or documentation. Just type

in what you're looking for, and the portal will display relevant options.

- **Resource Groups:**
  - o Resources in Azure are organized into groups. A resource group is a logical container for related resources (like virtual machines, databases, and storage accounts). This organization simplifies management, billing, and permissions.

Resource Management

- **Creating and Managing Resources:**
  - o To create a new resource, click on "Create a resource" from the global navigation or the dashboard.
  - o Follow the guided process to configure and deploy the resource. Each service has its own set of options, but the process is designed to be intuitive and user-friendly.
- **Monitoring and Alerts:**
  - o Azure provides built-in monitoring tools that let you track the performance and health of your resources.
  - o Set up alerts to be notified about critical issues, such as resource utilization thresholds or service outages.

Real-World Example: Setting Up a New Account and Creating a Resource Group

Let's walk through a practical, step-by-step example of how a small business owner might set up their Azure account and organize their cloud resources.

Step 1: Create Your Azure Account

1. **Sign Up:**
   - Visit azure.microsoft.com and click on "Start free."
   - Fill in your personal details and verify your identity using your phone number.
   - Provide your credit card information to complete the account creation process.
2. **Access the Azure Portal:**
   - Once your account is activated, sign in to the Azure Portal with your new credentials.
   - Spend a few minutes exploring the default dashboard to see how resources are displayed.

Step 2: Set Up Your Subscription and Manage Billing

1. **View Your Subscription:**
   - o In the Azure Portal, navigate to "Cost Management + Billing."
   - o Review your subscription details, including the free credits provided to new users.
2. **Set Up a Budget:**
   - o Create a budget by defining a spending limit and configuring alerts to notify you if your costs approach that threshold.
3. **Explore Usage Insights:**
   - o Familiarize yourself with the usage and cost analysis tools available in the billing section.

Step 3: Create a Resource Group

1. **Navigate to Resource Groups:**
   - o From the main menu or the dashboard, click on "Resource groups."
   - o Click "+ Create" to start a new resource group.
2. **Configure the Resource Group:**
   - o **Name:** Choose a descriptive name that reflects the purpose (e.g., "RetailResources" for a retail chain's online services).
   - o **Region:** Select a region that is closest to your customers to ensure low latency.

- o **Tags (Optional):** Add tags for better organization and cost tracking (e.g., "department: retail," "project: online-store").

3. **Create the Group:**
   - o Review your configuration and click "Create." Your resource group is now ready to organize your Azure services.

4. **Add Resources:**
   - o You can now start adding resources (such as virtual machines, databases, or storage accounts) to this group, which will help you manage them as a unified entity.

Conclusion

Setting up your Azure account and learning to navigate the Azure Portal is the first crucial step in your cloud journey. In this chapter, we introduced you to the process of creating an Azure account, managing your subscription and billing, and navigating the intuitive interface of the Azure Portal. Through a real-world example, we demonstrated how even a small business can quickly set up a new account and organize its cloud resources using resource groups.

By mastering these foundational steps, you're well on your way to developing and deploying cloud solutions with confidence. The skills learned here will pave the way for exploring Azure's extensive suite of services in the upcoming chapters.

Key Takeaways

1. **Account Setup:**
   o Creating an Azure account is straightforward, with a simple sign-up process that includes identity verification and payment setup.

2. **Subscription and Billing:**
   o Understanding how to manage your subscriptions, set budgets, and monitor costs is essential for optimizing cloud spending.

3. **Navigating the Azure Portal:**
   o The Azure Portal's dashboards, menus, and resource groups make it easy to manage and organize your cloud resources.

4. **Real-World Application:**
   o A step-by-step guide to setting up a resource group illustrates how to logically organize cloud resources, making management and cost tracking more efficient.

CHAPTER 4

Understanding Azure Regions, Availability Zones, and Data Residency

Introduction

As businesses increasingly migrate to the cloud, understanding how and where your data and applications are hosted becomes critical. Microsoft Azure, like other major cloud providers, operates a global network of data centers organized into regions and Availability Zones. In this chapter, we'll explain what these terms mean and why they are essential for planning a robust, resilient, and compliant cloud infrastructure. We'll cover how geographic distribution can help reduce latency, improve redundancy, and ensure regulatory compliance. Finally, a real-world example will illustrate how deploying a website across multiple regions can enhance high availability and disaster recovery capabilities.

Azure Regions

Azure regions are geographical areas that consist of multiple data centers located close to each other. Each region is designed to offer high-speed connectivity and redundancy within its boundaries. Azure currently spans many regions worldwide, allowing organizations to choose locations that best serve their user base. Selecting the right region can reduce latency—ensuring faster response times for your applications—and can also play a key role in regulatory compliance by keeping data within specific geographic borders.

Availability Zones

Within many Azure regions, data centers are further segmented into Availability Zones. An Availability Zone is a physically separate facility within a region that has its own power, cooling, and networking infrastructure. This design ensures that even if one zone experiences a failure, the others can continue to operate normally. By deploying resources across multiple Availability Zones, you can safeguard your applications against localized failures and achieve a higher level of resiliency.

Key Benefits

- **Reduced Latency:** By choosing a region close to your end-users, you minimize the distance data must travel, resulting in faster application performance.
- **Increased Redundancy:** Deploying applications across multiple Availability Zones ensures that if one zone goes offline, the others can maintain service continuity.
- **Regulatory Compliance:** Certain industries and regions have strict data residency laws that require data to be stored in a specific geographical area. Azure regions allow you to select a location that meets these legal requirements.

Planning for Latency, Redundancy, and Compliance

Addressing Latency

When planning your cloud deployment, consider where your users are located. Hosting your application in a region that is geographically close to your target audience minimizes the delay in data transmission, which is particularly important for real-time applications such as streaming services or online gaming platforms.

Ensuring Redundancy

Redundancy is the ability of a system to continue operating even if one or more components fail. In Azure, redundancy is achieved by deploying your applications across multiple Availability Zones within a region. This setup ensures that your application can withstand hardware failures, network disruptions, or even entire data center outages without significant downtime.

Meeting Compliance Requirements

Data residency and regulatory compliance are often major considerations, especially for industries like healthcare, finance, or government. Different countries and regions have laws that dictate where data must be stored and how it should be managed. Azure allows you to choose regions that meet these regulatory requirements, ensuring that your cloud solutions are compliant with local laws and industry standards.

Data Residency

Data residency refers to the physical location where your data is stored. It is an important factor for compliance with various legal and regulatory frameworks. By choosing an Azure region that aligns with your jurisdiction's requirements, you can ensure that sensitive data is stored within specified boundaries.

Regulatory Compliance

Many industries are subject to strict regulations regarding data privacy and security. For example:

- **Healthcare:** Regulations like HIPAA in the United States require that patient data is stored and managed in a secure and compliant manner.
- **Finance:** Financial institutions must adhere to standards such as PCI-DSS, which dictate how payment data is handled.
- **Government:** Government agencies often need to store data within national borders and follow stringent security protocols.

Azure's global infrastructure is designed with these compliance needs in mind. By selecting the appropriate regions and leveraging built-in compliance certifications, organizations can build cloud solutions that meet even the most rigorous regulatory standards.

Real-World Example: Deploying a Website Across Multiple Regions

Imagine a retail chain that operates both physical stores and an online shopping platform. To provide the best possible user experience, the company needs its website to be fast, reliable, and resilient against regional disruptions.

The Challenge

Previously, the website was hosted on a single data center, resulting in:

- **High Latency:** Customers located far from the data center experienced slower load times.
- **Risk of Downtime:** If the data center encountered issues, the website would go offline, impacting sales and customer satisfaction.

- **Compliance Concerns:** The company needed to ensure that customer data was stored in accordance with regional data residency laws.

The Azure Solution

1. **Choosing Multiple Regions:** The retail chain decided to deploy the website in two Azure regions—one in North America and another in Europe. This geographical distribution ensured that customers in both regions experienced lower latency and faster load times.

2. **Leveraging Availability Zones:** Within each region, the company deployed its web services across multiple Availability Zones. This configuration meant that if one zone experienced an outage, the services in the other zones would continue to operate, ensuring continuous availability.

3. **Data Residency Compliance:** By carefully selecting regions that met local data residency regulations, the retail chain was able to ensure that customer data was stored in compliance with all applicable laws.

4. **Global Load Balancing:** The company implemented a global load balancer to

route user requests to the nearest region. In the event of a regional outage, the load balancer automatically redirected traffic to the backup region, minimizing downtime.

The Outcome

- **Improved Performance:** Customers experienced faster website load times due to the reduced latency from being served by a nearby region.
- **Enhanced Resilience:** The multi-region, multi-zone deployment provided robust redundancy, ensuring that the website remained available even during localized failures.
- **Regulatory Compliance:** Data residency and compliance requirements were met, reducing legal risks and building customer trust.

Conclusion

Understanding Azure's regions, Availability Zones, and data residency is crucial for designing a cloud infrastructure that is fast, resilient, and compliant. By leveraging the global reach of Azure, businesses can reduce latency, improve service continuity, and meet regulatory requirements. The real-world example of a retail chain deploying a website across multiple regions demonstrates how these concepts translate into practical benefits, from enhanced performance to robust disaster recovery.

As you progress through this book, keep in mind that the strategic use of Azure's global infrastructure is a key factor in building reliable, scalable, and secure cloud solutions. With this foundation, you're now ready to explore more advanced aspects of developing and deploying cloud solutions on Azure.

Key Takeaways

1. **Regions and Availability Zones:**
   o Azure regions are geographical areas with multiple data centers, and Availability Zones within these regions offer additional redundancy.
2. **Latency, Redundancy, and Compliance:**
   o Selecting the right regions helps reduce latency, provides redundancy through multiple zones, and ensures compliance with data residency regulations.
3. **Real-World Impact:**

- o Deploying a website across multiple regions enhances performance and resilience, ensuring high availability and robust disaster recovery.

4. **Strategic Infrastructure Planning:**

- o Understanding and utilizing Azure's global infrastructure is critical for designing effective cloud solutions that meet both business and regulatory needs.

CHAPTER 5

Introduction to Azure Compute Options

Introduction

At the heart of every cloud solution is compute—the ability to run your applications and process data. Microsoft Azure offers a range of compute services designed to meet different needs, from full control over operating systems to completely managed, serverless environments. In this chapter, we will explore three core Azure compute options in simple terms: Virtual Machines, Azure App Services, and Azure Functions. We'll discuss when each option is most appropriate based on workload requirements and cost considerations. Finally, we'll illustrate these differences with a real-world example comparing the deployment of a web application on a Virtual Machine versus using Azure App Services for easier management.

Azure provides several ways to run your code in the cloud, and choosing the right option is key to building efficient and cost-effective solutions.

Virtual Machines (VMs)

What They Are:

- Virtual Machines are essentially complete computers hosted in the cloud.
- You have full control over the operating system, installed software, and configuration.
- VMs give you the flexibility to run legacy applications, custom software, or any workload that requires a specific environment.

Advantages:

- **Flexibility:** Customize the environment exactly as you need it.
- **Control:** Install any software, manage security patches, and configure system settings.
- **Isolation:** Each VM runs independently, which is useful for applications requiring strict separation.

Considerations:

- **Management Overhead:** You're responsible for operating system updates, security patches, and scaling manually or with additional tools.
- **Cost:** VMs can be more expensive if they are underutilized, as you pay for the full machine regardless of load.

Azure App Services

What It Is:

- Azure App Services is a Platform as a Service (PaaS) that allows you to deploy web applications and APIs without worrying about the underlying hardware or operating system.
- It abstracts the infrastructure management so you can focus on writing code.

Advantages:

- **Ease of Use:** Quickly deploy and update your web application with minimal setup.
- **Automatic Scaling:** The service automatically handles scaling to match traffic without manual intervention.

- **Integrated Management:** Features like custom domains, SSL, and continuous deployment are built into the platform.

Considerations:

- **Less Customization:** While you get many built-in features, you have less control over the underlying environment compared to VMs.
- **PaaS Model:** Ideal for applications that can operate within the provided framework but may not suit every specialized workload.

Azure Functions

What They Are:

- Azure Functions offer a serverless computing model, meaning you run your code in response to events without managing the infrastructure.
- This service is ideal for tasks that need to run on demand, such as processing data when a file is uploaded or responding to a web request.

Advantages:

- **Cost-Effective:** You only pay for the execution time of your code, making it highly cost-efficient for sporadic or burst workloads.
- **Automatic Scaling:** Azure automatically scales the number of function instances based on the volume of incoming events.
- **Simplicity:** Focus on writing small pieces of code (functions) without worrying about servers or scalability.

Considerations:

- **Stateless Nature:** Azure Functions are best suited for stateless operations, as any state must be stored externally.
- **Cold Starts:** For infrequent functions, there can be a slight delay (a cold start) when the function is triggered after being idle.

When to Choose Each Compute Option

Choosing the right compute service in Azure depends on your specific needs:

- **Choose Virtual Machines if:**
  - You need complete control over the operating system and installed software.

- o You are running legacy applications or workloads that require a specific environment.
- o You have the resources to manage the infrastructure (updates, security, scaling).

- **Choose Azure App Services if:**
  - o You want to deploy web applications or APIs quickly without managing the underlying servers.
  - o You prefer an environment that automatically scales based on traffic.
  - o You value simplicity and integrated features like continuous deployment, custom domains, and SSL management.

- **Choose Azure Functions if:**
  - o You have event-driven workloads or need to run code on demand.
  - o You want a cost-effective solution where you pay only for the actual execution time.
  - o Your tasks are stateless, or you can manage state externally.

Real-World Example: Deploying a Web Application

Let's compare two scenarios: deploying a web application on a Virtual Machine versus using Azure App Services.

Scenario 1: Deployment on a Virtual Machine

Setup:

- A company deploys its online store on an Azure Virtual Machine running a full operating system.
- The development team is responsible for configuring the server, installing the necessary software (like a web server and application runtime), and setting up security updates.
- Scaling the application requires manually provisioning additional VMs and setting up load balancers.

Pros:

- Full control over the environment allows for custom configurations and specialized software installations.
- Ideal for applications that require specific operating system settings or legacy software.

Cons:

- Higher management overhead: IT staff must continuously update and secure the VM.
- Scaling can be complex and time-consuming, potentially leading to downtime during peak periods.

Scenario 2: Deployment Using Azure App Services

Setup:

- The same online store is deployed using Azure App Services.
- Developers simply upload their web application code via a continuous deployment pipeline.
- Azure automatically manages the underlying infrastructure, applies updates, and scales the application based on traffic.

Pros:

- Reduced management overhead: The platform handles updates, scaling, and infrastructure security.
- Faster deployment cycles allow for quick updates and new feature rollouts.
- Built-in features like load balancing, auto-scaling, and integrated monitoring improve overall performance and reliability.

Cons:

- Less granular control over the underlying environment, which may not suit every specialized workload.
- Certain legacy applications might require adjustments to work within the PaaS model.

Outcome

For many web applications, especially those designed with modern development practices in mind, Azure App Services offers a compelling solution. The ease of use, automated scaling, and integrated management features often lead to reduced operational costs and improved agility compared to deploying on Virtual Machines. However, organizations with highly specialized requirements or legacy systems may still find Virtual Machines to be the better choice.

Conclusion

Azure's compute options provide the flexibility to choose the best fit for your workload—whether you need full control with Virtual Machines, a managed platform with Azure App Services, or an event-driven approach with Azure Functions. Understanding the strengths and trade-offs of each option is key to designing a cloud solution that balances performance, cost, and operational efficiency.

In this chapter, we covered:

- What Virtual Machines, Azure App Services, and Azure Functions are.

- The advantages and considerations for each compute option.
- A real-world example comparing a web application deployment on a Virtual Machine versus Azure App Services.

Armed with this knowledge, you can make informed decisions about which Azure compute service best meets your project's requirements, ensuring that your applications run efficiently and cost-effectively in the cloud.

Key Takeaways

1. **Virtual Machines:**
   - Provide full control and customization but require more management effort and manual scaling.
2. **Azure App Services:**
   - Offer a fully managed platform that simplifies deployment, scaling, and updates, ideal for web applications.
3. **Azure Functions:**
   - Are perfect for event-driven, stateless workloads where you pay only for execution time.
4. **Choosing the Right Option:**

o Your decision should be based on the specific needs of your workload, cost considerations, and management capabilities.

5. **Real-World Impact:**

o A comparison of deploying a web application on a Virtual Machine versus using Azure App Services illustrates how platform choice can affect scalability, management, and overall performance.

PART II

DEVELOPING CLOUD SOLUTIONS WITH AZURE

CHAPTER 6

Azure Storage Solutions Simplified

Introduction

In any cloud solution, efficient and reliable data storage is a critical component. Microsoft Azure provides a diverse array of storage options tailored to meet different needs—ranging from unstructured data and file shares to messaging and persistent disk storage. In this chapter, we'll break down Azure's primary storage services in a clear, jargon-free manner. You'll learn about Blob Storage, File Storage, Queue Storage, and Disk Storage, understand how each option works, and discover how to choose the right storage solution based on your specific requirements. We will also illustrate these concepts with a real-world example of migrating an on-premises file storage system to Azure Blob Storage, highlighting the benefits of scalability and cost savings.

Azure offers several storage services, each optimized for different types of data and workloads. Let's explore the key storage options available on Azure:

Blob Storage

What   It   Is:
Blob Storage is designed for storing large amounts of unstructured data, such as text or binary data. This includes files like documents, images, videos, backups, and log files.

Key Characteristics:

- **Scalability:**
  Blob Storage is highly scalable, capable of handling petabytes of data without compromising performance.
- **Cost   Efficiency:**
  It offers different tiers (hot, cool, and archive) that allow you to balance cost and access speed based on how frequently you need to access your data.
- **Accessibility:**
  Data in Blob Storage can be accessed via HTTP/HTTPS, making it ideal for web applications and media streaming.

File Storage

What **It** **Is:**

Azure File Storage provides fully managed file shares in the cloud that are accessible using the Server Message Block (SMB) protocol. This makes it easy to lift and shift applications that rely on file storage from on-premises environments to Azure.

Key Characteristics:

- **Simplicity:**
  It works like a traditional file server, allowing you to map the file share as a network drive on your operating system.
- **Collaboration:**
  Multiple users and applications can access and share files simultaneously.
- **Integration:**
  Ideal for legacy applications that expect a file-based storage system.

Queue Storage

What **It** **Is:**

Queue Storage provides a reliable messaging solution for decoupling application components. It allows you to store large numbers of messages that can be processed asynchronously.

Key Characteristics:

- **Asynchronous   Communication:**
  Helps in building scalable, decoupled applications by enabling components to communicate via messages without requiring immediate responses.
- **Reliability:**
  Ensures messages are stored safely until they are processed, which is particularly useful for scenarios where tasks need to be handled in the background.
- **Scalability:**
  Supports a high volume of messages, making it suitable for distributed systems and microservices architectures.

Disk Storage

What   It   Is:
Disk Storage provides persistent, high-performance storage that is used primarily with Azure Virtual Machines. It offers managed disks that deliver high throughput and low latency for critical applications.

Key Characteristics:

- **Durability:**
  Data is automatically replicated to protect against hardware failures.

- **Performance:**
Available in different performance tiers to suit various workloads, from basic disk needs to high-performance, enterprise-grade storage.

- **Integration:**
Seamlessly integrates with Virtual Machines, allowing for consistent performance across your applications.

Choosing the Right Storage Solution

Selecting the appropriate storage solution in Azure depends on the type of data you need to store, how often you need to access it, and the performance requirements of your applications. Here's a quick guide to help you decide:

- **Use Blob Storage if:**
  - You need to store large amounts of unstructured data such as images, videos, logs, or backups.
  - You require different storage tiers to optimize costs based on data access frequency.
  - Your application needs to serve media content or documents over the web.
- **Use File Storage if:**

- You need a shared file system that multiple users or applications can access via standard file protocols (SMB).
- You're migrating legacy applications that expect a file-based storage system.
- You require a simple, managed file share solution without having to manage your own file servers.

- **Use Queue Storage if:**
  - You need a reliable way to decouple application components and enable asynchronous processing.
  - Your workload involves high volumes of messages that need to be processed independently.
  - You're building microservices or distributed systems where tasks are handled asynchronously.

- **Use Disk Storage if:**
  - You require persistent storage for Azure Virtual Machines.
  - Your applications demand high I/O performance, such as databases or critical transactional systems.
  - You need a reliable and scalable disk solution with performance guarantees.

Real-World Example: Migrating On-Premises File Storage to Azure Blob Storage

Imagine a mid-sized company that has been managing its file storage using on-premises servers. Over time, the company has experienced several challenges:

- **Limited   Scalability:** The on-premises file server is reaching its storage capacity, making it difficult to support the growing volume of data.
- **High   Maintenance   Costs:** Managing physical hardware, backups, and upgrades has become increasingly expensive.
- **Operational   Complexity:** The IT team is spending more time on server maintenance and less on strategic initiatives, hindering innovation.

The Azure Blob Storage Solution

To overcome these challenges, the company decides to migrate its file storage to Azure Blob Storage. Here's how the process unfolds:

1. **Assessment and Planning:**

- The IT team evaluates the current storage usage and identifies the types of files stored (documents, images, backups, etc.).
- They plan the migration by mapping the on-premises file structure to Blob Storage, choosing the appropriate access tiers (hot for frequently accessed data and cool for archival purposes).

2. Migration Process:

- **Data**   **Transfer:** The team uses Azure's migration tools and services (such as Azure Data Box or AzCopy) to transfer large volumes of data from the on-premises server to Azure Blob Storage.
- **Configuration:** Blob Storage is configured with access policies to ensure that data is secure and cost-effective. For instance, data that is rarely accessed is moved to the cool tier, reducing storage costs.
- **Testing:** After migration, the IT team tests access to the data using web-based interfaces and APIs to confirm that files are available and can be served quickly to end-users.

3. Benefits Realized:

- **Scalability:** Azure Blob Storage provides virtually unlimited storage, so the company can grow without worrying about capacity constraints.

- o **Cost** **Savings:** With the pay-as-you-go model and different access tiers, the company reduces its storage costs significantly.

- o **Operational** **Efficiency:** The IT team no longer needs to manage physical hardware, freeing them up to focus on strategic initiatives and innovation.

- o **Improved** **Accessibility:** Files stored in Azure Blob Storage can be accessed from anywhere in the world, improving collaboration and customer service.

Conclusion

Azure Storage Solutions offer a versatile and cost-effective way to manage data in the cloud. Whether you need to store vast amounts of unstructured data, share files across your organization, facilitate asynchronous communication, or provide high-performance storage for virtual machines, Azure has a solution tailored to your needs. This chapter provided a clear overview of Blob Storage, File Storage, Queue Storage, and Disk Storage, along with practical guidance on how to choose the right option based on workload and cost considerations.

The real-world example of migrating an on-premises file storage system to Azure Blob Storage illustrates how businesses can achieve scalability, reduce operational costs, and improve data accessibility—all critical factors for thriving in today's digital landscape.

As you continue your journey into Azure, you'll discover how these storage solutions integrate with other Azure services to form a robust, end-to-end cloud solution.

Key Takeaways

1. **Azure Storage Options:**
   - o **Blob Storage:** Ideal for large amounts of unstructured data with flexible access tiers.
   - o **File Storage:** Provides managed, shared file systems using standard protocols.
   - o **Queue Storage:** Enables reliable, asynchronous messaging between application components.
   - o **Disk Storage:** Offers high-performance, persistent storage for virtual machines.
2. **Choosing the Right Solution:**

o   Select based on data type, access frequency, performance needs, and cost considerations.

3. **Real-World Impact:**

o   Migrating to Azure Blob Storage can dramatically improve scalability, reduce costs, and simplify data management for businesses.

4. **Strategic Cloud Adoption:**

o   Understanding and utilizing Azure's storage solutions is a key step in building a modern, efficient cloud infrastructure.

CHAPTER 7

Networking in Azure Made Simple

Introduction

In the cloud, networking is the backbone that connects your applications and services, ensuring seamless communication between on-premises systems and cloud resources. Microsoft Azure offers a robust yet accessible set of networking features designed to make it easy to create secure, efficient, and scalable networks. In this chapter, we introduce Azure networking fundamentals in a clear, jargon-free manner. We will explore virtual networks, subnets, and various connectivity options such as VPN and ExpressRoute. Additionally, we'll address essential security considerations to keep your network safe. Finally, a real-world example demonstrates how to set up a secure hybrid network between an on-premises office and Azure.

Understanding Azure Virtual Networks

What Are Virtual Networks?

- **Definition:**

  An Azure Virtual Network (VNet) is a logical representation of your own network in the cloud. It allows you to securely connect Azure resources, such as virtual machines, web apps, and databases, while isolating them from external networks.

- **Key Features:**

  o **Isolation:** VNets create a private network environment within Azure.

  o **Connectivity:** They enable communication among your resources and can be connected to your on-premises network.

  o **Customizable IP Addressing:** You can define your own IP address range, create subnets, and control network traffic.

Subnets

- **Definition:**

  Subnets divide a virtual network into smaller, manageable segments. Each subnet can host specific resources and help organize your network logically.

- **Benefits:**

  o **Improved Security:** Segregate different types of resources (e.g., front-end web servers vs. back-end databases) to apply tailored security policies.

- o **Better Traffic Management:** Control the flow of network traffic between subnets using Network Security Groups (NSGs) and routing rules.

Connectivity Options: VPN and ExpressRoute

VPN Gateway

- **What It Is:** A VPN Gateway allows you to create secure, encrypted connections between your on-premises network and your Azure Virtual Network over the public internet.
- **Benefits:**
  - o **Security:** Data is encrypted during transit.
  - o **Cost-Effective:** It's an affordable way to extend your on-premises network to the cloud.
  - o **Flexibility:** Suitable for a variety of scenarios, including remote work and hybrid cloud deployments.

ExpressRoute

- **What It Is:** ExpressRoute provides a dedicated, private connection between your on-premises infrastructure and Azure data centers, bypassing the public internet entirely.
- **Benefits:**
  - **Enhanced Performance:** Lower latency and higher reliability compared to VPN connections.
  - **Security:** More secure due to a private, direct connection.
  - **Scalability:** Ideal for large enterprises with significant data transfer needs or strict compliance requirements.

Security Considerations in Azure Networking

Security is a crucial aspect of any network—especially when bridging on-premises and cloud environments. Here are some best practices:

- **Network Segmentation:** Use subnets and Network Security Groups (NSGs) to control and restrict traffic between different parts of your network.

- **Encryption:**
  Always encrypt data in transit. VPN Gateways use robust encryption protocols to safeguard data, while ExpressRoute offers enhanced security through private connectivity.

- **Access   Controls:**
  Implement strict identity and access management (IAM) policies. Use Azure Active Directory (Azure AD) for centralized access control and multi-factor authentication (MFA).

- **Regular   Monitoring:**
  Continuously monitor network traffic and configurations using Azure Monitor and Azure Security Center to detect and respond to threats promptly.

Real-World Example: Setting Up a Secure Hybrid Network

Imagine a mid-sized company with a central office that hosts its internal systems on-premises. The company wants to extend its network to Azure to support additional cloud-based applications, improve disaster recovery, and provide remote access for employees. Here's how they set up a secure hybrid network:

Step 1: Create an Azure Virtual Network

- **Define the VNet:**
  The IT team creates a Virtual Network in Azure with a custom IP address range that does not overlap with the on-premises network.
- **Divide into Subnets:**
  The VNet is segmented into multiple subnets, such as one for web applications and another for backend services.

Step 2: Establish a VPN Gateway Connection

- **Deploy a VPN Gateway:**
  In the Azure Portal, the team deploys a VPN Gateway to enable encrypted communication between Azure and the on-premises network.
- **Configure the On-Premises VPN Device:**
  The company's IT staff configures the existing on-premises VPN device to connect to the Azure VPN Gateway.
- **Establish a Connection:**
  Once configured, a secure VPN tunnel is established, allowing data to flow securely between on-premises systems and Azure resources.

Step 3: Enhance Security and Manage Traffic

- **Apply Network Security Groups:**
  NSGs are set up on each subnet to control inbound and outbound traffic, ensuring only authorized access is permitted.

- **Implement Monitoring:**
  Azure Monitor and Security Center are configured to track network activity and alert the IT team to any unusual patterns.

Outcome

By setting up this hybrid network, the company achieved:

- **Seamless Connectivity:**
  Employees can securely access both on-premises and cloud applications as if they were part of the same network.

- **Improved Disaster Recovery:**
  Critical data and applications are now hosted in both environments, ensuring continuity in case of an outage at one location.

- **Enhanced Security:**
  The encrypted VPN tunnel and segmented network design protect sensitive data from potential threats.

Conclusion

Azure networking is designed to be powerful yet accessible, enabling you to build secure, scalable, and high-performing network architectures without overwhelming complexity. By understanding virtual networks, subnets, and connectivity options like VPN and ExpressRoute, you can extend your on-premises infrastructure to the cloud confidently. The real-world example of setting up a secure hybrid network illustrates how these concepts translate into tangible benefits, such as enhanced security, improved performance, and robust disaster recovery.

As you continue through this book, you'll build on these networking fundamentals to explore more advanced cloud solutions and integrations on Azure.

Key Takeaways

1. **Virtual Networks and Subnets:**
   - Azure Virtual Networks create private cloud environments, while subnets allow for logical segmentation and better traffic management.

2. **Connectivity Options:**

   o VPN Gateways provide secure, encrypted connections over the internet, whereas ExpressRoute offers a dedicated private connection for improved performance and security.

3. **Security Best Practices:**

   o Implement network segmentation, encryption, strict access controls, and continuous monitoring to safeguard your cloud environment.

4. **Real-World Impact:**

   o Setting up a secure hybrid network between an on-premises office and Azure enables seamless connectivity, enhanced security, and effective disaster recovery.

CHAPTER 8

Managing Azure Resources with Azure Resource Manager (ARM)

Introduction

Managing your cloud resources can quickly become complex as the number of services and applications grows. Microsoft Azure addresses this challenge with Azure Resource Manager (ARM), a powerful platform for deploying, organizing, and managing your cloud assets in a consistent and scalable way. In this chapter, we will explore the key components of ARM—including templates, resource groups, tags, and policies—and explain best practices for organizing your resources. To make these concepts tangible, we'll walk through a real-world example where a multi-tier application is deployed using an ARM template, simplifying ongoing management and updates.

Azure Resource Manager is the deployment and management service for Azure. It provides a unified management layer that enables you to create, update, and delete resources in your Azure account. ARM organizes resources into logical groups and enforces policies and permissions across these groups.

ARM Templates

- **What They Are:** ARM templates are JSON files that define the infrastructure and configuration for your Azure environment. They enable you to declare the desired state of your resources in a consistent, repeatable, and automated manner.
- **Key Benefits:**
  - **Automation:** Templates allow you to deploy entire environments with a single command.
  - **Consistency:** By using templates, you ensure that every deployment is identical, eliminating human error.
  - **Version Control:** ARM templates can be stored in source control, allowing you to track changes and roll back if necessary.

Resource Groups

- **What They Are:**
  A resource group is a container that holds related Azure resources such as virtual machines, storage accounts, databases, and more. Grouping resources logically simplifies management, access control, and cost tracking.

- **Why They Matter:**
  - **Organization:** Keep resources for a specific project or application together for easier monitoring and management.
  - **Lifecycle Management:** You can deploy, update, or delete all resources in a group simultaneously, which is particularly useful for applications with a defined lifecycle.

Tags

- **What They Are:**
  Tags are metadata elements that you attach to Azure resources. They consist of key-value pairs that provide additional information about the resource.

- **Benefits:**
  - **Cost Management:** Tags help you track costs by department, project, or environment.

- o **Resource Organization:** They enable you to filter and sort resources, making it easier to manage large environments.

Policies

- **What They Are:** Azure Policies are rules that help enforce organizational standards and compliance requirements. They can restrict the types of resources that can be deployed, enforce tagging, or control resource locations.
- **Benefits:**
  - o **Governance:** Policies ensure that resources adhere to your organization's security and management standards.
  - o **Compliance:** They help maintain compliance with industry regulations and internal guidelines by automatically auditing and enforcing configurations.

Best Practices for Resource Organization

Organizing your Azure resources effectively is crucial for maintaining a scalable, secure, and cost-effective cloud environment. Here are some best practices:

1. **Use Resource Groups Wisely:**
   o Group resources by project, application, or lifecycle stage (e.g., development, testing, production).
   o Keep related resources together to simplify updates and deletions.

2. **Adopt a Consistent Tagging Strategy:**
   o Develop a standard set of tags (e.g., "Department," "Project," "Environment") and enforce their usage across all resources.
   o Regularly audit tags to ensure compliance and consistency.

3. **Implement Azure Policies:**
   o Define and enforce policies that govern resource deployment, such as allowed regions, naming conventions, and tagging requirements.
   o Use policy initiatives to group related policies and apply them to resource groups or subscriptions.

4. **Version Control Your ARM Templates:**

- o Store ARM templates in a source control system (e.g., Git) to track changes over time and collaborate with team members.
- o Test templates in a non-production environment before applying them in production.

Real-World Example: Deploying a Multi-Tier Application Using an ARM Template

To illustrate how ARM simplifies resource management, let's walk through a real-world scenario where a company deploys a multi-tier web application using an ARM template.

Scenario Overview

A mid-sized e-commerce business wants to deploy a new online store. The application architecture includes:

- **Web Tier:** Hosting the front-end application.
- **Application Tier:** Running business logic.
- **Database Tier:** Storing customer and transaction data.

The goal is to deploy these components in a coordinated manner, ensuring that updates and management can be done consistently across the environment.

Step-by-Step Deployment

1. **Define the ARM Template:**

   An ARM template is created to define all the necessary resources. Below is a simplified snippet of such a template:

```json
{
  "$schema":
"https://schema.management.azure.com/sche
mas/2019-04-01/deploymentTemplate.json#",
  "contentVersion": "1.0.0.0",
  "parameters": {
    "resourceGroupLocation": {
      "type": "string",
      "defaultValue": "eastus",
      "metadata": {
        "description": "Location for all
resources."
      }
    },
```

```json
    "webAppName": {
      "type": "string",
      "metadata": {
        "description": "Name of the Web
App."
      }
    }
  },
  "variables": {
    "appServicePlanName":
"myAppServicePlan"
  },
  "resources": [
    {
      "type": "Microsoft.Web/serverfarms",
      "apiVersion": "2021-02-01",
      "name":
"[variables('appServicePlanName')]",
      "location":
"[parameters('resourceGroupLocation')]",
      "sku": {
        "Tier": "Standard",
        "Name": "S1"
      },
      "properties": {}
    },
    {
      "type": "Microsoft.Web/sites",
      "apiVersion": "2021-02-01",
```

```
      "name":
"[parameters('webAppName')]",
      "location":
"[parameters('resourceGroupLocation')]",
      "dependsOn": [

"[resourceId('Microsoft.Web/serverfarms',
variables('appServicePlanName'))]"
      ],
      "properties": {
        "serverFarmId":
"[resourceId('Microsoft.Web/serverfarms',
variables('appServicePlanName'))]"
      }
    },
    {
      "type": "Microsoft.Sql/servers",
      "apiVersion": "2021-02-01-preview",
      "name": "mySqlServer",
      "location":
"[parameters('resourceGroupLocation')]",
      "properties": {
        "administratorLogin": "sqladmin",
        "administratorLoginPassword":
"P@ssw0rd!"
      }
    },
    {
```

```
        "type":
"Microsoft.Sql/servers/databases",
        "apiVersion": "2021-02-01-preview",
        "name": "mySqlServer/myDatabase",
        "dependsOn": [
          "mySqlServer"
        ],
        "properties": {
          "collation":
"SQL_Latin1_General_CP1_CI_AS",
          "maxSizeBytes": "1073741824",
          "sampleName": "AdventureWorksLT"
        }
      }
    ],
    "outputs": {
      "webAppUrl": {
        "type": "string",
        "value":          "[concat('https://',
parameters('webAppName'),
'.azurewebsites.net')]"
      }
    }
}
```

Explanation:

- o **Parameters:**

  Define configurable inputs, such as location and web app name.

- o **Variables:**

  Simplify resource naming (e.g., the App Service Plan).

- o **Resources:**

  Deploy a multi-tier architecture that includes an App Service Plan, a Web App, and a SQL Database.

- o **Outputs:**

  Provide the URL for the deployed web app for quick access after deployment.

2. **Deploy the Template:**

Using the Azure Portal or Azure CLI, the IT team deploys the ARM template into a resource group. For example, using Azure CLI:

```bash
```

```
az deployment group create --resource-
group MyResourceGroup --template-file
azuredeploy.json
```

This command creates and configures all defined resources automatically.

3. **Manage and Update:**

With the ARM template in source control, future updates (such as scaling out the web app or modifying database configurations) can be managed through versioned changes to the template. The entire application can be redeployed with consistent configuration, simplifying maintenance and updates.

Benefits of Using ARM Templates

- **Consistency and Repeatability:** Every deployment is identical, ensuring that your infrastructure remains standardized.
- **Automation:** Reduce manual errors by automating the creation and configuration of resources.
- **Simplified Management:** Updates, scaling, and rollbacks can be handled by updating the template and redeploying it, streamlining ongoing management.

Conclusion

Azure Resource Manager (ARM) is a powerful tool for deploying and managing your cloud infrastructure in a consistent, automated, and scalable way. By using ARM templates, resource groups, tags, and policies, you can efficiently organize your resources and maintain a well-governed cloud environment. The real-world example of deploying a multi-tier application using an ARM template highlights how this approach simplifies management and updates, enabling organizations to focus more on innovation and less on manual infrastructure management.

As you continue your journey with Azure, mastering ARM will provide you with a strong foundation to build, deploy, and maintain robust cloud solutions.

Key Takeaways

1. **ARM Templates:**
   o Define your infrastructure as code in a consistent and automated manner.
2. **Resource Groups:**

- o Organize related resources to simplify management, cost tracking, and lifecycle management.

3. **Tags and Policies:**
   - o Use metadata and governance rules to maintain a secure and compliant environment.

4. **Real-World Impact:**
   - o Deploying a multi-tier application with an ARM template demonstrates how to simplify resource management and enable rapid, consistent updates.

5. **Automation and Scalability:**
   - o ARM empowers you to manage complex environments with minimal manual intervention, paving the way for efficient cloud operations.

CHAPTER 9

Securing Your Azure Environment

Introduction

Security is a top priority in the cloud, especially when you're handling sensitive data such as healthcare records, financial information, or personal user data. Microsoft Azure provides a robust set of tools and best practices to help you secure your cloud environment and meet strict regulatory standards. In this chapter, we will introduce essential security practices in Azure, focusing on identity and access management with Azure Active Directory (Azure AD) and how to utilize Azure Security Center to monitor your environment and ensure compliance. We'll also illustrate these concepts with a real-world example of how a cloud-based healthcare application can be secured to meet HIPAA requirements.

Identity and Access Management with Azure Active Directory

What Is Azure Active Directory?

Azure Active Directory (Azure AD) is Microsoft's cloud-based identity and access management service. It serves as the backbone for controlling who can access your resources in Azure. With Azure AD, you can manage users, groups, and roles, making sure that only the right people have access to your applications and data.

Key Features of Azure AD

- **Centralized User Management:** Create and manage user accounts in one place, making it easy to add new employees or revoke access when someone leaves.

- **Role-Based Access Control (RBAC):** Assign roles to users or groups that define what actions they can perform within Azure. For example, you might allow only administrators to create or modify resources, while other users can only view them.

- **Multi-Factor Authentication (MFA):** Enhance security by requiring users to verify their identity using a second factor, such as a text message or an authentication app. This extra step significantly reduces the risk of unauthorized access.

- **Single Sign-On (SSO):**
  With SSO, users can access multiple applications with one set of credentials, improving both security and user convenience.

Benefits for Your Environment

By using Azure AD, organizations can ensure that access to cloud resources is tightly controlled and monitored. This is particularly important for industries like healthcare, where data sensitivity is paramount and regulatory requirements demand strict access controls.

Utilizing Azure Security Center and Compliance Standards

What Is Azure Security Center?

Azure Security Center is a unified infrastructure security management system that provides advanced threat protection across your hybrid workloads in the cloud. It helps you:

- **Assess Your Security Posture:** Continuously analyze your Azure environment for vulnerabilities and configuration issues.

- **Provide Recommendations:** Offer actionable guidance on how to improve your security settings.

- **Automate Policy Enforcement:** Implement policies to ensure that your resources comply with industry standards and best practices.

How Azure Security Center Supports Compliance

Azure Security Center comes with built-in compliance assessments for several regulatory standards, including HIPAA (Health Insurance Portability and Accountability Act), PCI-DSS (Payment Card Industry Data Security Standard), and more. It provides:

- **Continuous Monitoring:** Alerts you to potential security issues before they become serious problems.

- **Reporting:** Generates compliance reports that simplify auditing and regulatory reviews.

- **Recommendations and Remediation:** Offers step-by-step instructions to remediate security gaps, ensuring that your environment meets the necessary standards.

Best Practices for Secure Cloud Environments

- **Regular Security Assessments:** Use Azure Security Center to perform continuous security assessments, making sure your configurations remain optimal as your environment evolves.

- **Implement Automated Alerts:** Set up automated alerts for suspicious activities or configuration changes to quickly respond to potential security incidents.

- **Enforce Strict Access Controls:** Combine Azure AD's RBAC with security policies in Security Center to restrict access and reduce the risk of insider threats.

- **Data Encryption:** Encrypt sensitive data both at rest and in transit to ensure that even if data is intercepted, it remains protected.

Imagine a healthcare provider that has moved its patient management and appointment scheduling systems to the cloud. Given the sensitive nature of healthcare data and the strict requirements of HIPAA, securing this environment is not just a best practice—it's a necessity.

Step 1: Secure Identity and Access

- **Azure AD for User Management:** The healthcare provider uses Azure AD to manage access to the application. Each employee is assigned a role based on their responsibilities (e.g., doctors, nurses, administrative staff), ensuring that users only have access to the data they need.
- **Multi-Factor Authentication:** MFA is enabled for all users, adding an extra layer of security by verifying identities before granting access.

Step 2: Monitor and Protect the Environment

- **Azure Security Center Implementation:** The provider deploys Azure Security Center to continuously monitor the environment. The tool automatically assesses the configuration of resources, detects potential vulnerabilities, and provides recommendations to address any issues.

- **Compliance Reporting:** Azure Security Center's compliance dashboard is used to generate reports that demonstrate adherence to HIPAA requirements. This simplifies audits and helps maintain regulatory compliance.

Step 3: Data Protection and Encryption

- **Encryption Policies:** All patient data stored in Azure is encrypted both at rest and in transit. This means that even if unauthorized access were attempted, the data would remain unreadable.

- **Access Controls:** Strict access controls ensure that only authorized personnel can access sensitive data. Any access is logged and monitored for unusual activity.

Outcome

Through these measures, the healthcare provider has built a robust, secure environment that not only meets HIPAA compliance but also instills confidence in both patients and regulatory bodies. By leveraging Azure AD for identity management and Azure Security Center for continuous monitoring and compliance, the provider minimizes risk and ensures that patient data is kept safe at all times.

Conclusion

Securing your Azure environment is a critical step in building reliable, compliant, and resilient cloud solutions. With tools like Azure Active Directory for managing user access and Azure Security Center for continuous monitoring and compliance enforcement, you can create a secure foundation for your cloud applications. Our real-world example of a healthcare application demonstrates how these tools work together to meet stringent regulatory requirements, such as HIPAA, while protecting sensitive data.

As you continue your journey in the Azure ecosystem, remember that security is an ongoing process. Regular assessments, strict access controls, and proactive monitoring are key to maintaining a secure cloud environment that can adapt to evolving threats and compliance standards.

Key Takeaways

1. **Azure Active Directory:**
   - Provides centralized identity and access management with features like RBAC, MFA, and SSO.

2. **Azure Security Center:**
   - Offers continuous security assessments, automated policy enforcement, and compliance reporting.

3. **Best Practices:**
   - Regularly monitor, encrypt, and enforce strict access controls to protect sensitive data.

4. **Real-World Impact:**
   - A cloud-based healthcare application can meet HIPAA requirements through the combined use of Azure AD and Azure Security Center, ensuring that patient data remains secure and compliant.

CHAPTER 10

Monitoring and Logging in Azure

Introduction

As businesses move their workloads to the cloud, ensuring that applications and infrastructure are running smoothly becomes a top priority. Monitoring and logging provide critical visibility into the health, performance, and security of your Azure environment. Without effective monitoring, issues can go unnoticed, leading to downtime, performance degradation, or security vulnerabilities.

Microsoft Azure offers a suite of powerful tools—such as **Azure Monitor**, **Log Analytics**, and **Application Insights**—to help track resource usage, detect anomalies, and troubleshoot problems efficiently. In this chapter, we'll explore how these tools work, discuss best practices for setting up alerts and dashboards, and walk through a real-world example of configuring monitoring for an e-commerce platform.

Azure Monitor

What It Is:
Azure Monitor is the central service for collecting, analyzing, and responding to telemetry data from your cloud and on-premises environments. It provides a comprehensive solution for performance monitoring, log aggregation, and alerting.

Key Capabilities:

- **Real-time Insights:** Continuously tracks metrics and logs from Azure resources.
- **Proactive Alerting:** Sends notifications based on predefined conditions.
- **Integration with Other Services:** Works seamlessly with Log Analytics and Application Insights.

Log Analytics

What It Is:
Log Analytics, part of Azure Monitor, allows you to collect

and query log data from multiple sources, including Azure services, virtual machines, and applications.

Key Capabilities:

- **Centralized Logging:** Consolidates logs from different services into a single repository.
- **Powerful Querying:** Uses Kusto Query Language (KQL) to extract insights from large datasets.
- **Troubleshooting:** Helps diagnose issues by correlating logs across services.

Example Query in Log Analytics:

```kusto
AzureActivity
| where ActivityStatus == "Failed"
| order by TimeGenerated desc
```

This query retrieves failed activity logs, helping administrators quickly identify issues.

Application Insights

What   **It**   **Is:**

Application Insights is an **application performance monitoring (APM)** tool designed to track the behavior and health of web applications.

Key Capabilities:

- **End-to-End Request Tracking:** Monitors how user requests flow through an application.
- **Performance Metrics:** Measures response times, failed requests, and server availability.
- **User Behavior Analysis:** Tracks user interactions to optimize application performance.

Example:

- **A web application experiences high response times.** With Application Insights, developers can trace the delay to a slow database query and optimize it.

Setting Up Alerts and Dashboards

Alerts

Azure Monitor allows you to configure alerts based on various conditions. These alerts can notify teams via **email,**

SMS, or integrated services like Microsoft Teams and PagerDuty.

Common Alert Scenarios:

- **CPU usage exceeds 80% on a virtual machine.**
- **An application throws more than 10 errors in a minute.**
- **A database query takes longer than 3 seconds.**

Steps to Create an Alert:

1. Go to the **Azure Portal** and navigate to **Azure Monitor**.
2. Select **Alerts > New Alert Rule**.
3. Choose a **Target Resource** (e.g., a virtual machine, application, or storage account).
4. Set the **Condition** (e.g., CPU usage > 80%).
5. Define an **Action Group** (who to notify and how).
6. Click **Create Alert**.

Dashboards

Dashboards provide a **visual representation** of key performance indicators (KPIs) across your environment.

Steps to Create a Dashboard:

1. In the **Azure Portal**, navigate to **Dashboards**.

2. Click + **New Dashboard**.

3. Add **Tiles** such as CPU utilization graphs, application response times, and active alerts.

4. Customize the layout to display the most important data at a glance.

Dashboards are particularly useful for **network operations centers (NOCs),** where teams monitor infrastructure in real time.

Real-World Example: Monitoring an E-Commerce Platform

Scenario

A growing e-commerce company runs its online store on **Azure App Services** with a **SQL Database** backend. They need a **monitoring solution** to ensure:

- The website remains **available and responsive**.
- Transactions **complete successfully**.
- Issues are **detected and resolved quickly**.

Step 1: Set Up Azure Monitor

- **Enable Azure Monitor** for all resources, including the web app, database, and storage accounts.
- Configure key **performance metrics**, such as request count, response time, and database latency.

Step 2: Implement Application Insights

- **Enable Application Insights** for the web application.
- Track:
    - **User traffic patterns** to identify peak hours.
    - **Failed requests** to detect application errors.
    - **Transaction times** to ensure the checkout process is smooth.

Example Insights:

- If a **product page takes more than 5 seconds to load**, an alert is triggered.
- If the **checkout process fails for more than 2% of transactions**, a **developer is notified immediately**.

Step 3: Configure Log Analytics

- Collect logs from the **web app, database, and security logs**.
- Set up a **query to track failed logins**, identifying potential security threats.

- Correlate logs to **detect dependencies causing slowdowns** (e.g., a slow API call).

Example Log Analytics Query:

```kusto
kusto
```

```
requests
| where success == false
| summarize count() by operation_Name
```

This query helps identify which operations are failing most often.

Step 4: Set Up Alerts and Dashboards

- Create an **alert for high response times** (e.g., if response time exceeds 3 seconds for more than 5 minutes).
- Set up **real-time dashboards** showing order volume, page load times, and active alerts.
- Integrate alerts with **Microsoft Teams** so that the operations team gets instant notifications.

Outcome

By implementing these monitoring and logging solutions, the e-commerce company benefits from: ✓ **Early Issue Detection:** The team is notified of issues before customers are   impacted.

✓ **Faster Troubleshooting:** Log Analytics and Application Insights   pinpoint   performance   bottlenecks.

✓ **Better User Experience:** Dashboards help proactively maintain   site   speed   and   uptime.

✓ **Increased Security:** Log monitoring helps detect potential security threats.

Conclusion

Effective monitoring and logging are **essential** for running a smooth and secure cloud environment. With **Azure Monitor, Log Analytics, and Application Insights**, you can track resource performance, detect anomalies, and troubleshoot issues in real time.

By implementing **alerts and dashboards**, you gain **full visibility** into your environment, ensuring that applications remain available and responsive. The real-world example of **an e-commerce platform** illustrates how Azure's monitoring tools can **detect issues before they impact customers**, helping businesses maintain **high uptime and optimal performance**.

As you continue your Azure journey, mastering monitoring and logging will help you build **resilient, high-performing cloud applications** that can scale with your business needs.

Key Takeaways

1. **Azure Monitor:**
   - Provides a **centralized solution** for monitoring Azure resources.
2. **Log Analytics:**
   - Aggregates and **queries logs** to identify trends and troubleshoot issues.
3. **Application Insights:**
   - Tracks **application performance** and **user behavior** in real time.
4. **Alerts and Dashboards:**
   - Enable proactive monitoring and **automated issue detection**.
5. **Real-World Impact:**

- ○ Monitoring an **e-commerce platform** ensures **high availability, quick issue resolution, and better customer experiences**.

PART III

BUILDING AND DEPLOYING SOLUTIONS ON AZURE

CHAPTER 11

Automating Deployments with Azure DevOps

Introduction

Modern software development requires speed, efficiency, and reliability. Organizations must deploy new features rapidly without sacrificing quality, security, or stability. **Azure DevOps** provides a powerful set of tools to automate software development and deployment processes, enabling teams to deliver applications with confidence.

This chapter explores **Continuous Integration (CI) and Continuous Deployment (CD)** pipelines, automated testing, and how Azure DevOps can streamline software delivery. We'll also walk through a real-world example where an e-commerce company reduced deployment time from **weeks to hours** using a fully automated CI/CD pipeline.

What is Azure DevOps?

Azure DevOps is a **suite of services** that provides everything needed for modern software development, including:

- **Azure Repos** – A version control system for tracking changes in your code.
- **Azure Pipelines** – A CI/CD tool for building, testing, and deploying applications automatically.
- **Azure Test Plans** – Automated testing tools to ensure application quality.
- **Azure Artifacts** – A package management system to store and distribute code dependencies.

By using Azure DevOps, teams can **automate deployments, ensure code quality, and scale applications effortlessly**.

Building CI/CD Pipelines Using Azure DevOps

What is CI/CD?

- **Continuous Integration (CI):**
  - Developers frequently merge code changes into a shared repository.

- o Each change triggers an automated build and test process to catch errors early.
- **Continuous Deployment (CD):**
  - o Code that passes testing is automatically deployed to production.
  - o Reduces manual intervention and speeds up delivery.

By implementing **CI/CD**, businesses can deploy features faster, reduce human errors, and maintain high application quality.

Step 1: Setting Up an Azure DevOps Pipeline

Azure Pipelines automates the CI/CD process by **building, testing, and deploying** applications. It supports various platforms, including **.NET, Node.js, Python, and Docker**.

Step-by-Step Guide: Creating a CI/CD Pipeline

1. **Create a New Azure DevOps Project:**
   - o Sign in to **Azure DevOps** (dev.azure.com).
   - o Click **New Project**, enter a name, and select Git as the version control system.
2. **Set Up a Repository:**

o Use **Azure Repos** to store your application's source code.

o Clone the repository locally and push your code.

3. **Define a Build Pipeline:**

o Go to **Pipelines > New Pipeline**.

o Select **GitHub/Azure Repos** as the source.

o Choose a **template** or define a pipeline using YAML.

4. **Configure Build Steps:**

o Example **YAML Build Pipeline** for a Node.js web app:

```yaml
yaml


trigger:
  - main
pool:
  vmImage: 'ubuntu-latest'
steps:
  - task: NodeTool@0
    inputs:
      versionSpec: '14.x'
  - script: npm install
    displayName:              'Install
Dependencies'
  - script: npm test
    displayName: 'Run Tests'
  - script: npm run build
```

```
displayName: 'Build Application'
```

5. **Run the Pipeline:**

- o The pipeline **automatically runs on each commit**, ensuring that only error-free code is merged.

Step 2: Integrating Automated Tests

Testing is **critical** to ensure reliability before deployment.

- **Unit Tests:** Check individual components.
- **Integration Tests:** Verify that different services work together.
- **UI Tests:** Automate user interactions.

Adding Automated Tests to the Pipeline: Modify the YAML pipeline to include testing:

yaml

```
- script: npm test
  displayName: 'Run Automated Tests'
```

This ensures that only code that **passes tests** is deployed.

Step 3: Deploying the Application Automatically

After successful testing, the application can be deployed using **Azure App Service, Virtual Machines, Kubernetes, or Containers**.

Setting Up Continuous Deployment (CD)

1. **Define a Release Pipeline:**
   o Navigate to **Pipelines > Releases**.
   o Create a **New Release Pipeline**.
   o Select the **Azure App Service** or any other hosting option.

2. **Configure Deployment Stages:**
   o Example: **Deploy to Development** → **Test** → **Production**.
   o Use approval gates to control production releases.

3. **Automate Deployment Using YAML:**

```yaml
- task: AzureWebApp@1
  inputs:
    appType: 'webApp'
    appName: 'my-webapp'
    package:
'$(Build.ArtifactStagingDirectory)/app.zip'
```

This automatically deploys the application to **Azure App Service**.

4. **Enable Blue-Green Deployments (Optional):**
   - Reduce downtime by deploying to a **staging environment** before switching to production.
   - This allows rollback in case of issues.

Real-World Example: Automating Deployment for an E-Commerce Platform

Scenario

A **mid-sized e-commerce company** sells products online. The development team struggled with: ✘ **Manual deployments taking weeks**

✘ **Frequent production bugs**

✘ **Rollback issues during failures**

The company adopted **Azure DevOps** to automate deployments.

Solution

1. **Implemented CI/CD Pipeline:**

- o Developers pushed code to Azure Repos.
- o **CI process** ran unit and integration tests.
- o Code automatically **built and packaged**.

2. **Automated Deployment:**
   - o A release pipeline deployed code to **staging first**.
   - o Once approved, it was pushed to **production**.

3. **Monitoring & Rollback Plan:**
   - o **Application Insights** monitored performance.
   - o If an issue occurred, they could **instantly revert to the previous version.**

Outcome

✓ **Deployment time reduced from weeks to hours.**

✓ **Fewer production errors due to automated testing.**

✓ **Developers focused on features instead of deployments.**

Conclusion

Azure DevOps **transforms software deployment**, ensuring speed, reliability, and efficiency. By implementing **CI/CD pipelines, automated testing, and staged deployments**, teams can deliver updates **faster and with fewer errors**.

The **real-world example** of an e-commerce company shows how DevOps automation **eliminates deployment bottlenecks, improves quality, and accelerates time-to-market**.

Mastering Azure DevOps will **empower you to automate, scale, and optimize your cloud deployments**, ensuring that your applications remain resilient, secure, and high-performing.

Key Takeaways

1. **Azure DevOps Automates Deployments:**
   o Reduces manual effort and human errors.
2. **CI/CD Pipelines Improve Code Quality:**
   o Ensures only tested, working code reaches production.
3. **Automated Testing Is Essential:**
   o Prevents bugs and improves reliability.
4. **Release Pipelines Enable Fast & Safe Deployments:**
   o Supports **staged rollouts** and **blue-green deployments**.
5. **Real-World Impact:**

- o An **e-commerce company reduced deployment time from weeks to hours** using Azure DevOps.

CHAPTER 12

Developing Cloud Solutions with Azure App Services

Introduction

Azure App Services is one of the most powerful and user-friendly platforms for hosting web applications, REST APIs, and mobile backends in the cloud. It provides a **fully managed** environment where developers can focus on writing code instead of worrying about infrastructure, maintenance, and scaling.

In this chapter, we'll take a **deep dive** into Azure App Services, covering how to **create, deploy, and scale applications** effortlessly. We'll also explore **custom domains, SSL certificates, and security configurations** to ensure that applications remain accessible and secure. Finally, we'll illustrate these concepts with a **real-world example of deploying a personal blog or business website** using Azure App Services for a hassle-free setup.

What is Azure App Services?

Azure App Services is a **Platform as a Service (PaaS)** solution that allows developers to quickly build, deploy, and scale web applications without managing the underlying infrastructure. It supports a variety of programming languages, including **.NET, Python, Java, Node.js, PHP, and Ruby.**

Key Benefits of Azure App Services

✅ **Fully Managed Hosting** – No need to manage servers or infrastructure.

✅ **Automatic Scaling** – Adjusts resources dynamically based on demand.

✅ **Built-in Security** – Supports authentication, role-based access, and encryption.

✅ **Custom Domains & SSL** – Easily secure and personalize application URLs.

✅ **Continuous Deployment** – Integrates with **Azure DevOps, GitHub, Bitbucket**, and other CI/CD tools.

Creating and Deploying Applications on Azure App
Services

Step 1: Creating an Azure App Service

To start, we need to **provision an App Service** in Azure.

1. **Go to the Azure Portal** (portal.azure.com).
2. Click **"Create a resource"** → Select **"Web App"**.
3. Enter the following details:
   - **App Name**: Choose a unique name (e.g., `mywebapp123`).
   - **Subscription**: Select the appropriate subscription.
   - **Resource Group**: Create a new group or use an existing one.
   - **Publish Type**: Choose **Code** (for direct deployment) or **Docker Container** if using containers.
   - **Runtime Stack**: Choose a programming language (e.g., Python, Node.js, .NET).
   - **Operating System**: Select **Linux** or **Windows**.
   - **Region**: Choose a region closest to your users.
4. Click **"Review + Create"**, then **"Create"**.

Step 2: Deploying Your Application

Once the App Service is created, you can **deploy your application** using multiple methods:

✅ **Azure DevOps or GitHub Actions** (CI/CD integration).

✅ **FTP/SFTP** for direct file uploads.

✅ **Azure CLI or Azure Portal** for manual deployments.

✅ **VS Code or Visual Studio** with Azure extensions.

Deploying via GitHub Actions (Recommended for CI/CD)

1. In the **Azure Portal**, navigate to your **App Service** → Select **Deployment Center**.
2. Choose **GitHub** and connect your repository.
3. Configure a **GitHub Actions** workflow (automates deployments on every code change).
4. Click **Save**, and the deployment will be triggered automatically.

Step 3: Scaling Applications

Scaling is **critical** for applications that experience fluctuating traffic. Azure App Services offers **two types of scaling**:

- **Vertical Scaling (Scaling Up)** – Increasing CPU, memory, or upgrading to a higher service plan.
- **Horizontal Scaling (Scaling Out)** – Adding multiple instances of the application to handle more traffic.

Configuring Auto-Scaling

1. In the **Azure Portal**, navigate to your **App Service**.
2. Go to **Scale Out (App Service Plan)**.
3. Enable **Auto-Scaling** and configure **rules** such as:
   - Scale up when CPU usage > 70%.
   - Scale down when traffic drops.

Auto-scaling ensures your application remains **highly available** without unnecessary costs.

Configuring Custom Domains and SSL

Adding a Custom Domain

By default, Azure App Services provides a URL like `mywebapp123.azurewebsites.net`. To use a **custom domain**, follow these steps:

1. Buy a domain from a **domain registrar** (e.g., GoDaddy, Namecheap).
2. In **Azure Portal**, navigate to your App Service → **Custom Domains**.
3. Add the **new domain** and follow the verification steps.
4. Update your **DNS records** to point to Azure's IP address.

Enabling SSL for Secure HTTPS Connections

Securing your application with **SSL/TLS** is essential for encrypting user data and improving trust. Azure offers:

✅ **Free App Service Managed Certificates** (for basic SSL).

✅ **Custom SSL Certificates** (if purchased externally).

Steps to Enable HTTPS:

1. Navigate to your **App Service** → **TLS/SSL Settings**.
2. Enable **HTTPS Only** (forces all traffic over HTTPS).
3. Upload your **SSL Certificate** (if using a custom one).

4. Bind the SSL certificate to your **custom domain**.

With SSL enabled, your website will now serve secure **HTTPS traffic** (`https://yourdomain.com`).

Real-World Example: Deploying a Personal Blog or Business Website

Scenario

A freelancer wants to **host a personal blog** without dealing with server management. They choose **Azure App Services** for its ease of use and scalability.

Step 1: Create an App Service

- The freelancer **creates a new App Service** in Azure.
- They select **WordPress on Linux** (pre-configured template).
- They choose a **Basic Plan** to minimize costs.

Step 2: Deploy the Blog

- They **connect their GitHub repository** containing the blog's code.

- **Azure DevOps automatically deploys** the website on each code change.

Step 3: Set Up a Custom Domain & SSL

- They **purchase a domain** (myportfolio.com).
- They add the domain to Azure and **enable free SSL**.

Step 4: Enable Auto-Scaling

- They configure **auto-scaling** so the site handles more traffic when needed.

Outcome

🏃 **Fast Setup** – The blog was live in minutes.

🔒 **Secure & Reliable** – SSL ensures safe browsing.

📈 **Scalable** – The site adapts to traffic spikes.

Conclusion

Azure App Services is a **powerful and flexible** hosting solution for web and mobile applications. With **automatic scaling, custom domains, SSL support, and CI/CD**

integration, it simplifies cloud development while ensuring security and high availability.

The **real-world example of deploying a personal blog** showcases how **anyone—from freelancers to businesses— can leverage Azure App Services for an effortless and scalable hosting solution.**

By mastering these concepts, you can confidently develop, deploy, and manage cloud-based applications **without managing infrastructure manually.**

Key Takeaways

1. **Azure App Services** is a **fully managed** platform for web and mobile apps.
2. **Multiple Deployment Options** – Use GitHub, Azure DevOps, FTP, or Azure CLI.
3. **Automatic Scaling** ensures high availability during traffic spikes.
4. **Custom Domains & SSL** enhance security and branding.
5. **Real-World Impact** – A **freelancer** deployed a secure blog in **minutes** without server management.

CHAPTER 13

Serverless Computing with Azure Functions

Introduction

In traditional cloud computing, applications run on **virtual machines (VMs) or containers**, requiring **manual scaling, infrastructure management, and cost monitoring**. **Serverless computing** eliminates these concerns by automatically managing **resource allocation and scaling**, allowing developers to focus purely on writing code.

Azure Functions, Microsoft's serverless computing platform, enables developers to build **event-driven applications** that run only when triggered, significantly reducing operational overhead and cost.

In this chapter, we will explore **serverless architectures**, **triggers and bindings**, and the **cost benefits of serverless computing**. We'll also demonstrate **how to build a real-world data processing pipeline** that triggers automatically when a file is uploaded to Azure Storage.

Traditional vs. Serverless Architectures

Feature	Traditional Cloud Computing (VMs, Containers)	Serverless Computing (Azure Functions)
Infrastructure Management	Requires provisioning and managing VMs or containers.	No infrastructure to manage—fully automated.
Scaling	Manual or auto-scaling based on pre-defined rules.	Automatically scales based on demand.
Cost Model	Pay for **allocated resources**, even when idle.	Pay **only for execution time** (per request).
Use Case	Suitable for **always-on** applications.	Best for **event-driven workloads** (e.g., API calls, file processing, message handling).

With **serverless computing, you never pay for idle time—** functions run **only when triggered.**

How Azure Functions Work

Azure Functions are small units of code that execute in response to events, making them **ideal for automating workflows** without managing infrastructure.

Key Concepts in Azure Functions

✅ **Triggers** – Define when a function should execute (e.g., HTTP request, database update, file upload).
✅ **Bindings** – Connect functions to external services (e.g., Azure Blob Storage, Cosmos DB).
✅ **Consumption-based Pricing** – Pay only when the function is executed.

Triggers and Bindings in Azure Functions

Triggers: What Starts a Function?

A **trigger** is an event that starts an Azure Function. Some common triggers include:

Trigger Type	Description	Example Use Case
HTTP Trigger	Executes when an HTTP request is received.	Web APIs, chatbots, webhook listeners.
Blob Storage Trigger	Fires when a new file is uploaded to Azure Blob Storage.	Automated image resizing, file processing.
Queue Storage Trigger	Runs when a message is added to an Azure Queue.	Background processing of jobs.
Timer Trigger	Runs at scheduled intervals (e.g., every 5 minutes).	Automated cleanup tasks, scheduled reports.
Cosmos DB Trigger	Fires when data changes in a Cosmos DB database.	Real-time analytics, database event processing.

Example: An **Azure Function with an HTTP Trigger**

```
python
```

```python
import logging
import azure.functions as func

def    main(req:    func.HttpRequest)    ->
func.HttpResponse:
    logging.info("HTTP    function    received    a
request.")
    return    func.HttpResponse("Hello,    Serverless
World!")
```

Bindings: Connecting to External Services

Bindings make it easy to connect functions to other Azure services without writing boilerplate code.

- **Input Bindings**: Fetch data from external sources (e.g., retrieve a file from Blob Storage).
- **Output Bindings**: Send processed data to external services (e.g., store results in a database).

Example: An **Azure Function with a Blob Storage Trigger and Output Binding**

```python
python

import logging
import azure.functions as func
```

```
def main(myblob: func.InputStream, outputBlob:
func.Out[str]) -> None:
    logging.info(f"Processing                 file:
{myblob.name}")

    # Read file content
    file_content = myblob.read().decode("utf-8")

    # Modify content and save to output blob
    modified_content = file_content.upper()
    outputBlob.set(modified_content)
```

✓ **Input Binding:** `myblob` fetches the uploaded file.

✓ **Output Binding:** `outputBlob` saves the modified content in another blob.

Cost Benefits and Scaling Advantages of Serverless Computing

Cost Efficiency: Pay Only for Execution Time

With **Azure Functions' Consumption Plan**, you are only billed   for:

✓ **Execution Time** – The duration of function execution.

✓ **Number of Executions** – Total function invocations.

✓ **Memory Usage** – Resources consumed during execution.

Example:

- Running a VM for **24 hours** costs **$50/month**.
- Running a function **only when triggered** costs **$5/month** (90% savings).

Automatic Scaling

✓ No need to configure load balancers—Azure **automatically scales** functions based on demand.
✓ Functions can scale **from zero to thousands of concurrent executions** in milliseconds.

Real-World Example: Building a Data Processing Pipeline with Azure Functions

Scenario

A **data analytics company** needs to **automatically process CSV files** uploaded to Azure Blob Storage. Each file contains sales data that needs to be:

✓ **Validated** (ensure correct format).

✓ **Stored** in an Azure SQL Database.

✓ **Triggered automatically** when a file is uploaded.

Step 1: Create an Azure Function with a Blob Trigger

1. Open **Azure Portal** → Navigate to **Functions App** → Click **Create**.
2. Choose **Consumption Plan** (pay-per-use).
3. Select **Blob Storage Trigger** and link it to an existing **Azure Storage Account**.

Step 2: Write the Function to Process the File

python

```python
import logging
import azure.functions as func
import pandas as pd
import pyodbc

# Database connection details
```

```python
conn_str = "Driver={ODBC Driver 17 for SQL
Server};Server=tcp:mydbserver.database.windows.
net;Database=mydb;Uid=myuser;Pwd=mypassword;"

def main(myblob: func.InputStream):
    logging.info(f"Processing        file:
{myblob.name}")

    # Read CSV file into Pandas DataFrame
    df = pd.read_csv(myblob)

    # Validate Data (check for missing values)
    if df.isnull().values.any():
        logging.error("Missing data detected.
Skipping file.")
        return

    # Insert data into Azure SQL Database
    conn = pyodbc.connect(conn_str)
    cursor = conn.cursor()
    for index, row in df.iterrows():
        cursor.execute("INSERT INTO SalesData
(Date, Product, Revenue) VALUES (?, ?, ?)",
                        row["Date"],
row["Product"], row["Revenue"])
    conn.commit()
    conn.close()

    logging.info("File successfully processed.")
```

✓ **Reads** **CSV** **file** using Pandas.

✓ **Validates data** before inserting it into Azure SQL.

✓ **Runs only when a new file is uploaded**, making it cost-effective.

Outcome

🚀 **Automation:** No manual intervention needed—function runs on **each** **file** **upload.**

💰 **Cost Savings:** No need for a constantly running server—**pays** **only** **for** **execution.**

📈 **Scalability:** Can process **hundreds of files in parallel.**

Conclusion

Azure Functions **simplify cloud development** by removing infrastructure management and **enabling event-driven applications** that **scale automatically.** With triggers and bindings, functions can seamlessly integrate with other Azure services.

The **real-world example** demonstrates how **a data processing pipeline** can be automated using **Blob Storage Triggers** and **Azure SQL integration.**

By leveraging **serverless computing**, organizations can **reduce costs, increase efficiency, and improve scalability** in modern cloud applications.

Key Takeaways

1. **Serverless Computing Eliminates Infrastructure Management**
   o No servers to maintain—**focus on code.**
2. **Azure Functions are Event-Driven**
   o **Triggered by HTTP requests, file uploads, database changes, etc.**
3. **Cost-Effective Pricing Model**
   o Pay **only when functions run** (no idle charges).
4. **Seamless Integrations**
   o Use **Triggers and Bindings** to connect to Azure services.
5. **Real-World Impact**
   o **A data processing pipeline** automates **file uploads → validation → database storage** without any manual intervention.

CHAPTER 14

Containers on Azure – Introduction to AKS (Azure Kubernetes Service)

Introduction

As applications grow in complexity, managing them efficiently becomes a challenge. Containerization has revolutionized modern application deployment, allowing developers to package applications with all their dependencies into a single, portable unit. However, running and scaling multiple containers across different environments requires **orchestration**—and that's where **Kubernetes** comes in.

Azure Kubernetes Service (AKS) is Microsoft's managed Kubernetes platform that simplifies container orchestration. It automates deployment, scaling, and management of containerized applications, making it easier to run microservices architectures, scale workloads, and maintain high availability.

In this chapter, we'll cover **containerization fundamentals, Kubernetes concepts, and how to set up an AKS cluster on Azure**. Finally, we'll walk through a **real-world example** of deploying a **microservices-based application** on AKS and scaling it to handle increased traffic.

Understanding Containers and Kubernetes

What is Containerization?

A **container** is a lightweight, standalone unit that encapsulates an application and its dependencies. Unlike traditional virtual machines (VMs), containers **share the host OS kernel**, making them more efficient and faster to deploy.

Why Use Containers?

✓ **Portability** – Run the same application anywhere (local, cloud, on-premises).

✓ **Efficiency** – Containers are lightweight and start quickly compared to VMs.

✓ **Scalability** – Containers can be easily replicated to handle more users.

✓ **Consistency** – Avoid "it works on my machine" problems by packaging dependencies together.

Popular Container Technologies:

- **Docker** – The most widely used container runtime.
- **Containerd** – A lightweight runtime used under Kubernetes.
- **Podman** – A rootless alternative to Docker.

What is Kubernetes?

Kubernetes is an **open-source container orchestration platform** that manages the deployment, scaling, and operations of containers.

Core Kubernetes Concepts

Component	Description
Pods	The smallest deployable unit in Kubernetes, containing one or more containers.
Nodes	Worker machines (VMs) that run containerized workloads.

Component	Description
Cluster	A group of nodes that run applications and workloads.
Deployments	Define how applications should be deployed and updated.
Services	Manage network access to Pods (e.g., expose an app on the internet).
Ingress	Controls external access to services using HTTP(S) routing.
Auto-Scaling	Automatically scales the number of running containers based on demand.

Setting Up and Managing an AKS Cluster

Step 1: Creating an AKS Cluster

Using Azure Portal

1. Navigate to **Azure Portal** → Click **Create a Resource** → Select **Azure Kubernetes Service**.
2. Enter the **cluster name** and choose a **resource group**.
3. Select **Region** (closest to your users).

4. Choose **Node Size and Count**:

   o **Standard_B2s** (for small workloads).

   o **Standard_D4s_v3** (for production workloads).

5. Enable **RBAC (Role-Based Access Control)** for security.

6. Click **Create** – Azure will provision the cluster in a few minutes.

Using Azure CLI

For those who prefer automation, use **Azure CLI** to create an AKS cluster:

```bash
az aks create --resource-group MyResourceGroup -
-name MyAKSCluster --node-count 2 --enable-
addons monitoring --generate-ssh-keys
```

✓ Creates a cluster with **2 nodes**.

✓ Enables **monitoring** for real-time metrics.

✓ Generates **SSH keys** for secure access.

Step 2: Deploying an Application to AKS

1. Install kubectl (Kubernetes CLI)

bash

```
az aks install-cli
```

✓ `kubectl` is the command-line tool for interacting with Kubernetes clusters.

2. Connect to AKS

bash

```
az aks get-credentials --resource-group MyResourceGroup --name MyAKSCluster
```

✓ Fetches cluster credentials, allowing you to run `kubectl` commands.

3. Deploy a Sample Application

bash

```
kubectl create deployment myapp --image=nginx
kubectl expose deployment myapp --type=LoadBalancer --port=80
```

✓ Deploys an **Nginx container** inside AKS. ✓ Exposes the application via an **Azure Load Balancer**.

To check the status:

```
bash
```

```
kubectl get services
```

Step 3: Scaling the Application

AKS supports **manual** and **automatic scaling** to handle traffic spikes.

Manually Scale Pods
```
bash
```

```
kubectl scale deployment myapp --replicas=5
```

✓ Increases the number of running **containers** from **1 to 5**.

Enable Auto-Scaling
```
bash
```

```
kubectl autoscale deployment myapp --cpu-percent=50 --min=2 --max=10
```

✓ Scales the application **dynamically** between **2 and 10 replicas** based on **CPU usage**.

Step 4: Monitoring and Logging

To monitor AKS performance, enable **Azure Monitor**:

```bash
bash
```

```bash
az    aks    enable-addons    --resource-group
MyResourceGroup    --name    MyAKSCluster    --addons
monitoring
```

✓ Sends **logs and metrics** to **Azure Monitor**.

Check real-time logs:

```bash
bash
```

```bash
kubectl logs -f deployment/myapp
```

Real-World Example: Deploying a Microservices-Based
Application on AKS

Scenario

A **fintech company** is launching a **payment processing
platform**.   The   application   consists   of:
✓ **Auth Service** – Handles user authentication.

✔ **Payment API** – Processes transactions.

✔ **Database Service** – Stores user and transaction data.

Challenges:

✘ The system must **handle thousands of transactions per second.**

✘ **Manual scaling** is too slow for high traffic spikes.

✘ Security must be **tight** to protect financial data.

Solution: Deploying the Application on AKS

Step 1: Deploy Each Microservice

Each service is **containerized** and deployed using Kubernetes.

Example **deployment file (auth-service.yaml):**

```yaml
apiVersion: apps/v1
kind: Deployment
metadata:
  name: auth-service
spec:
```

```
replicas: 3
selector:
  matchLabels:
    app: auth-service
template:
  metadata:
    labels:
      app: auth-service
  spec:
    containers:
    - name: auth-service
      image: myrepo/auth-service:latest
      ports:
      - containerPort: 8080
```

✓ Deploys **3 instances** of the authentication service.

bash

```
kubectl apply -f auth-service.yaml
```

Step 2: Expose the Services via Ingress

To route traffic to the correct microservice, use **Ingress**:

yaml

```
apiVersion: networking.k8s.io/v1
kind: Ingress
metadata:
```

```
    name: payment-ingress
spec:
  rules:
  - host: payments.myapp.com
    http:
      paths:
      - backend:
          service:
            name: payment-api
            port:
              number: 80
```

bash

```
kubectl apply -f payment-ingress.yaml
```

✓ Routes **payments.myapp.com** requests to **payment-api**.

Step 3: Enable Auto-Scaling

bash

```
kubectl autoscale deployment payment-api --cpu-
percent=60 --min=3 --max=15
```

✓ Automatically **scales up to 15 instances** during peak hours.

Conclusion

Azure Kubernetes Service (AKS) **simplifies container orchestration**, making it easier to **deploy, scale, and manage** containerized applications.

The **real-world fintech example** demonstrates how **AKS can dynamically scale microservices**, ensuring **high availability and performance**.

By mastering **AKS**, you can deploy **resilient, scalable, and cost-efficient** containerized applications on Azure.

Key Takeaways

1. **Containers Improve Portability** – Applications run **consistently across environments**.
2. **Kubernetes Manages Scaling & Load Balancing** – Handles **high-traffic workloads** efficiently.
3. **AKS Automates Infrastructure Management** – No need to manually configure servers.
4. **Real-World Impact** – A **fintech company scaled payments processing** to handle **thousands of transactions per second**.

CHAPTER 15

Alternative Container Options – Azure Container Instances and Service Fabric

Introduction

While **Azure Kubernetes Service (AKS)** is the go-to solution for running large-scale containerized applications, Azure offers other container services that may be more suitable for specific workloads. **Azure Container Instances (ACI)** and **Azure Service Fabric** provide **alternative ways to deploy and manage containers** without the complexity of a full Kubernetes cluster.

In this chapter, we will explore **ACI and Service Fabric**, compare them with **AKS**, and discuss **when to use each service**. We will also walk through a **real-world example of using Azure Container Instances (ACI) to run a short-lived batch job** for rapid processing.

Understanding the Differences Between ACI, Service Fabric, and AKS

Azure offers multiple container services, each optimized for different use cases. Below is a high-level comparison:

Feature	Azure Kubernetes Service (AKS)	Azure Container Instances (ACI)	Azure Service Fabric
Best For	Large-scale containerized apps	Short-lived workloads, simple apps	Stateful applications, microservices
Management	Requires managing cluster resources	Fully managed, serverless	Full control over infrastructure
Scaling	Auto-scaling across multiple nodes	Rapid provisioning, but no auto-scaling	Fine-grained scaling

Feature	Azure Kubernetes Service (AKS)	Azure Container Instances (ACI)	Azure Service Fabric
Use Cases	Web apps, APIs, microservices	Batch jobs, event-driven tasks	Stateful apps, IoT, messaging services
Complexity	High	Low	Medium-High
Networking	Full networking control	Public or private access	Advanced IP networking capabilities

When to Choose Each Service

- **Use AKS** when you need **full control** over a large-scale, distributed application with **auto-scaling, load balancing, and orchestration**.
- **Use ACI** for **fast, serverless container deployments** where you don't need to manage infrastructure—ideal for short-lived batch jobs or quick API hosting.
- **Use Service Fabric** when **building complex, stateful applications** that require **high availability, low latency, and enterprise-level reliability**.

Azure Container Instances (ACI) is a **serverless container solution** that allows you to run **single containers** without managing infrastructure. It is ideal for **quick, on-demand execution** of containerized workloads.

Key Features of ACI

✅ **Instant Start** – Deploy containers in seconds.

✅ **Serverless** – No need to provision or manage virtual machines.

✅ **Cost-Efficient** – Pay only for the seconds your container is running.

✅ **Integrated with AKS** – Offload some tasks from Kubernetes to ACI.

✅ **Public or Private Networking** – Containers can be exposed to the internet or kept private.

Common Use Cases for ACI

- **Batch Jobs & Event-Driven Tasks** – Data processing, scheduled tasks, video encoding.

- **API Hosting** – Quick, lightweight web services without infrastructure management.
- **Development & Testing** – Run isolated development environments.

What is Azure Service Fabric?

Azure Service Fabric is a **distributed systems platform** designed for running **stateful and stateless** applications at scale. Unlike AKS and ACI, Service Fabric is **not just a container orchestrator**—it is optimized for complex applications that require advanced networking, microservices, and service discovery.

Key Features of Service Fabric

✅ **Supports Containers and Non-Containerized Apps** – Run microservices in containers or as processes.

✅ **Built for Stateful Applications** – Ideal for applications needing **persistent state management**.

✅ **Automatic Failover** – Self-healing capabilities ensure reliability.

✅ **Multi-Cloud and Hybrid** – Can run in Azure, on-premises, or other cloud providers.

Common Use Cases for Service Fabric

- **Enterprise Microservices** – Large, complex applications that require high availability.
- **IoT and Edge Computing** – Processing large volumes of real-time data.
- **Financial Applications** – Mission-critical banking or stock market systems.

Real-World Example: Running a Short-Lived Batch Job on ACI

Scenario

A **data analytics company** needs to process **large CSV files** daily and extract key insights. Instead of **maintaining a VM** or **deploying a Kubernetes cluster**, they decide to use **Azure Container Instances (ACI)** to process each file on-demand and shut down automatically after completion.

Step 1: Create a Container Image

First, create a simple **Python script** (`process_csv.py`) that reads a CSV file, processes data, and outputs the results.

```python
import pandas as pd

# Read CSV file
df = pd.read_csv('/data/input.csv')

# Perform data transformation
df['Total'] = df['Quantity'] * df['Price']

# Save output
df.to_csv('/data/output.csv', index=False)

print("Processing completed successfully!")
```

Next, create a **Dockerfile** to containerize this script:

```dockerfile
FROM python:3.9
WORKDIR /app
COPY process_csv.py .
COPY input.csv /data/input.csv
RUN pip install pandas
CMD ["python", "process_csv.py"]
```

Build and push the image to **Azure Container Registry (ACR)**:

```bash
# Log in to Azure
az login

# Create a container registry
az acr create --resource-group MyResourceGroup -
-name MyACR --sku Basic

# Log in to the registry
az acr login --name MyACR

# Build and push the image
docker build -t myacr.azurecr.io/process-
csv:latest .
docker push myacr.azurecr.io/process-csv:latest
```

Step 2: Deploy the Container to ACI

Now that the container is built, deploy it to **Azure Container Instances (ACI)**.

```bash
az container create \
```

```
--resource-group MyResourceGroup \
--name csv-processor \
--image myacr.azurecr.io/process-csv:latest \
--cpu 1 --memory 1 \
--restart-policy Never
```

✓ This starts the container **only when needed**.
✓ Once processing completes, the container **automatically shuts down** (cost-efficient).

Step 3: Automate Execution with Azure Logic Apps

To **automate this batch job**, use **Azure Logic Apps**:

1. **Trigger:** Set up a Logic App to **monitor an Azure Storage Blob**.
2. **Action:** When a new CSV file is uploaded, automatically **invoke the ACI container**.
3. **Notification:** Once the processing completes, **send an email notification**.

Outcome

✅ **No need for VMs or Kubernetes clusters** – Runs only when needed.

✅ **Processing time reduced from hours to minutes**.

✅ **100% cost-efficient** – Pay only for execution time.

✅ **Easily scalable** – Increase CPU/memory for larger files.

Conclusion

Azure offers **multiple container options** beyond **AKS** to fit different workloads.

✓ **Azure Container Instances (ACI)** is the best choice for **serverless, short-lived workloads**, such as batch jobs and event-driven tasks.

✓ **Azure Service Fabric** is ideal for **stateful, enterprise-grade applications** that require advanced orchestration and fault tolerance.

✓ **AKS** remains the best solution for **large-scale, containerized applications** with complex microservices.

The **real-world example** demonstrated how **ACI can rapidly process large data files without infrastructure** management. This **serverless approach** ensures **cost efficiency, scalability, and automation**.

Mastering **Azure's container ecosystem** will empower you to choose the **right containerization strategy** for your applications.

Key Takeaways

1. **ACI is ideal for lightweight, serverless workloads** – Best for **batch jobs, quick deployments, and event-driven processing**.
2. **Service Fabric excels in stateful, high-availability applications** – Used for **financial systems, IoT, and large enterprise workloads**.
3. **AKS remains the best for full-scale container orchestration** – Provides **full Kubernetes capabilities**.
4. **Real-World Impact** – A **data analytics company automated CSV processing using ACI**, reducing operational complexity and cost.

CHAPTER 16

Data Solutions on Azure – Databases and Analytics

Introduction

Data is at the core of modern applications and businesses. Whether you're dealing with structured data in relational databases or unstructured big data for analytics, **Azure provides a comprehensive set of data services** to help you store, process, and analyze data efficiently.

Azure offers **managed relational databases (SQL Database), NoSQL solutions (Cosmos DB), big data storage (Data Lake)**, and **enterprise-scale analytics (Synapse Analytics)**. These services reduce the burden of infrastructure management, improve security, and scale seamlessly with business needs.

In this chapter, we will explore **Azure's core data solutions**, discuss **data migration and performance tuning strategies**, and walk through a **real-world example of** migrating a relational database to Azure SQL Database and using Synapse Analytics for business insights.

Overview of Azure's Core Data Services

1. Azure SQL Database (Managed Relational Database)

Azure SQL Database is a fully managed **relational database-as-a-service** **(DBaaS)** that offers high availability, security, and automated scaling.

Key Features:

✅ **Automatic Backups** – Point-in-time restore up to 35 days.

✅ **Scalability** – Scale vertically or add read replicas.

✅ **Built-in Security** – Advanced Threat Protection (ATP) and   encryption.

✅ **Serverless Option** – Pauses when inactive to save costs.

- Hosting **transactional applications** (e.g., banking, e-commerce).
- Migrating **on-prem SQL Server** workloads to the cloud.
- **Data warehousing** for analytics and reporting.

---

2. Azure Cosmos DB (NoSQL and Multi-Model Database)

Azure Cosmos DB is a **globally distributed NoSQL database** designed for high-speed, low-latency applications.

Key Features:

✅ **Multi-Model Support** – Supports **document, key-value, column-family, and graph databases**.

✅ **Global Distribution** – Multi-region replication with low-latency reads/writes.

✅ **Horizontal Scaling** – Automatically scales throughput and storage.

✅ **Guaranteed Performance** – Offers **single-digit millisecond** response times.

Use Cases:

- **IoT Applications** – Storing sensor data in real-time.
- **E-commerce & Personalization** – Powering product recommendations.
- **Real-time Analytics** – Processing high-velocity application logs.

---

3. Azure Data Lake (Big Data Storage & Analytics)

Azure Data Lake Storage (ADLS) is a **scalable storage service** optimized for **big data analytics**.

Key Features:

✅ **Optimized for Massive Datasets** – Handles petabytes of data.

✅ **Secure & Cost-Effective** – Fine-grained access controls and low-cost storage tiers.

✅ **Hadoop & Spark Integration** – Native compatibility with **Azure Synapse Analytics, Databricks, and HDInsight**.

- Storing **raw data for machine learning and AI**.
- **ETL (Extract, Transform, Load) Pipelines** for structured and unstructured data.
- **Data Lakehouse Architectures** integrating with **Synapse Analytics**.

---

4. Azure Synapse Analytics (Enterprise Data Warehouse & Analytics)

Azure Synapse Analytics (formerly SQL Data Warehouse) is a **unified analytics platform** that combines **big data processing, data warehousing, and real-time analytics**.

Key Features:

✅ **Massive Parallel Processing (MPP)** – Optimized for **complex queries on large datasets**.

✅ **Integrated with Power BI** – For real-time visualization and business intelligence.

✅ **PolyBase Support** – Query structured and unstructured data **without moving it**.

✅ **AI-Enhanced Analytics** – Supports **Apache Spark, ML, and data streaming**.

Use Cases:

- **Enterprise Reporting & BI Dashboards.**
- **Predictive Analytics & Machine Learning Pipelines.**
- **Processing Clickstream Data & Customer Insights.**

Data Migration and Performance Tuning

Migrating Databases to Azure

Migrating to the cloud can seem complex, but **Azure provides multiple tools** to streamline the process:

Migration Tool	Use Case
Azure Database Migration Service (DMS)	Migrating **on-prem SQL Server, Oracle, MySQL, and PostgreSQL** to Azure SQL Database.
Data Pipelines Factory	Moving large datasets into **Data Lake or Synapse Analytics**.

Migration Tool	Use Case
Cosmos DB Data Migration Tool	Importing NoSQL data from **MongoDB, SQL, CSV, or JSON** into Cosmos DB.

Performance Optimization Best Practices

For Azure SQL Database:

✓ **Use Elastic Pools** – Manage multiple databases efficiently.

✓ **Optimize Indexing** – Use **Azure SQL Advisor** to detect missing indexes.

✓ **Enable Query Performance Insights** – Identify **slow queries** and improve execution.

For Cosmos DB:

✓ **Choose the Right Partition Key** – Evenly distribute workload across partitions.

✓ **Enable Automatic Indexing** – Speeds up queries.

✓ **Optimize Throughput (RU/s)** – Scale reads/writes dynamically to reduce costs.

For Synapse Analytics:

✓ **Use Materialized Views** – Store pre-aggregated query results for faster performance.

✓ **Leverage Columnstore Indexes** – Optimized for analytical workloads.

✓ **Scale Compute Dynamically** – Adjust performance tiers based on query complexity.

Real-World Example: Migrating a Relational Database to Azure SQL and Using Synapse Analytics

Scenario

A **retail company** wants to migrate its on-premises **SQL Server database** to the cloud and use **Synapse Analytics** to analyze **sales trends and optimize inventory management**.

Step 1: Migrate the Database to Azure SQL

1. **Assess Compatibility**

    o   Use **Azure Migrate** to check database **schema compatibility**.

2. **Migrate the Data**

```bash
az dms create --resource-group RetailRG --name RetailDMS --sku-name Premium_4vCores
```

3. **Verify and Optimize**
   - Enable **geo-replication** for disaster recovery.
   - Use **Query Performance Insights** to tune queries.

Step 2: Load Data into Synapse Analytics for Business Intelligence

1. **Extract Data from Azure SQL**

```sql
SELECT * INTO sales_raw FROM sales_database
```

2. **Transform Data Using Synapse Pipelines**
   - Apply **currency conversion, tax calculations, and seasonal trends**.

3. **Generate Business Reports**

   o Use **Power BI** to create **real-time sales dashboards**.

Outcome

✦ **50% Faster Query Performance** – Optimized indexes & parallel execution.

● **30% Cost Savings** – Migrated from on-prem hardware to a scalable cloud model.

✓ **Real-Time Insights** – Sales managers track inventory instantly with Power BI.

Conclusion

Azure offers a **powerful ecosystem of data services** to help businesses store, process, and analyze their data efficiently. Whether you need a **relational database, a NoSQL solution, a big data platform, or enterprise analytics**, Azure provides scalable solutions that fit your workload.

The **real-world example** demonstrated how a **retail company migrated SQL Server to Azure SQL Database** and **leveraged Synapse Analytics** for real-time **business intelligence**—a common pattern for modern data-driven organizations.

By mastering **Azure's data solutions**, you can **optimize performance, reduce costs, and unlock valuable insights from your data**.

Key Takeaways

1. **Azure SQL Database** – Best for **transactional applications** and **relational workloads**.
2. **Azure Cosmos DB** – Ideal for **globally distributed, high-speed NoSQL applications**.
3. **Azure Data Lake** – Optimized for **big data storage and analytics**.
4. **Azure Synapse Analytics** – Best for **enterprise-scale data warehousing and reporting**.
5. **Real-World Impact** – A **retail company migrated SQL Server** to **Azure SQL Database & Synapse Analytics**, **reducing costs and improving data-driven decision-making**.

CHAPTER 17

AI and Machine Learning with Azure

Introduction

Artificial Intelligence (AI) and Machine Learning (ML) are transforming industries by enabling businesses to **automate processes, extract insights from data, and enhance user experiences**. Azure provides a **comprehensive suite of AI and ML services** that allow organizations to **build, train, and deploy AI models without requiring deep expertise in data science**.

In this chapter, we will explore **Azure Machine Learning, Cognitive Services, and Bot Services**—the key tools available for AI-powered applications. We will also walk through a **real-world example of creating a recommendation engine for an online store** using **Azure Machine Learning**.

Azure provides several **fully managed AI and ML services** to help developers and data scientists **build, train, and deploy intelligent applications.**

1. Azure Machine Learning (Azure ML)

Azure Machine Learning is a cloud-based platform that enables users to **train, deploy, and manage machine learning models at scale.**

Key Features:

✅ **AutoML** – Automates model selection and hyperparameter tuning.

✅ **Model Training & Deployment** – Supports both **notebook-based (Jupyter) and drag-and-drop (Designer)** development.

✅ **MLOps** – Automates ML lifecycle with CI/CD pipelines.

✅ **Scalability** – Train models on **CPU, GPU, or FPGA clusters.**

Use Cases:

- **Predictive analytics** (e.g., sales forecasting).

- **Anomaly detection** (e.g., fraud detection).
- **Recommendation engines** (e.g., personalized shopping experiences).

---

2. Azure Cognitive Services

Azure Cognitive Services provides **pre-built AI models** that allow developers to integrate AI capabilities **without extensive ML expertise**.

Key Features:

✅ **Vision** – Image recognition, object detection, and OCR.

✅ **Speech** – Speech-to-text, text-to-speech, and real-time translation.

✅ **Language** – Sentiment analysis, language detection, and text translation.

✅ **Decision** – AI-based recommendations and personalization.

Use Cases:

- **Customer Support Bots** – Using **Azure Speech & Language APIs**.

- **Automated Document Processing** – Extracting text from scanned documents.
- **Real-Time Translation** – Multilingual chat applications.

Example API Call for **Sentiment Analysis**:

```python
import requests

api_url = "https://api.cognitive.microsoft.com/text/analytics/v3.0/sentiment"
headers = {"Ocp-Apim-Subscription-Key": "YOUR_API_KEY"}
data = {"documents": [{"id": "1", "language": "en", "text": "I love this product!"}]}

response = requests.post(api_url, headers=headers, json=data)
print(response.json())  # Returns sentiment score (e.g., positive, neutral, negative)
```

3. Azure Bot Services

Azure **Bot Services** enables developers to build, test, and deploy intelligent chatbots that **engage with users** across various platforms.

Key Features:

✅ **Bot Framework SDK** – Create chatbots with pre-built NLP   capabilities.

✅ **Integration with Cognitive Services** – Improve bots with **speech recognition and natural language understanding**.

✅ **Multi-Platform Deployment** – Deploy bots to **Microsoft Teams, WhatsApp, Facebook Messenger, or custom websites**.

Use Cases:

- **E-commerce Support Bots** – Handle customer inquiries automatically.
- **Appointment Scheduling** – Automate bookings via chat interfaces.
- **HR Virtual Assistants** – Answer employee queries on policies and benefits.

Building and Deploying AI Models with Azure Machine Learning

Step 1: Setting Up an Azure ML Workspace

To start using **Azure Machine Learning**, follow these steps:

Using Azure Portal

1. **Go to Azure Portal** → Search for **Azure Machine Learning**.
2. Click **Create New Workspace**.
3. Fill in the details:
   - **Workspace Name**: `my-ml-workspace`
   - **Subscription**: Choose your Azure subscription.
   - **Resource Group**: Create or select an existing one.
   - **Region**: Choose the closest region.
4. Click **Create**.

Using Azure CLI

Alternatively, create a workspace using Azure CLI:

bash

```
az ml workspace create -n my-ml-workspace -g
MyResourceGroup --location eastus
```

✓ This sets up a cloud environment for **data storage, model training, and deployment**.

Step 2: Training a Machine Learning Model

Once the workspace is ready, we can train an ML model using **Azure ML SDK** in Python.

1. Install Azure ML SDK

bash

```
pip install azureml-sdk
```

2. Connect to the ML Workspace

python

```
from azureml.core import Workspace

ws = Workspace.from_config()
print(ws.name, "loaded successfully.")
```

3. Load and Preprocess Data

python

```
import pandas as pd

# Load dataset (e.g., customer purchases for a
recommendation engine)
df = pd.read_csv("customer_purchases.csv")

# Feature engineering (convert categorical data
to numerical)
df = pd.get_dummies(df, columns=['Category'])
```

4. Train a Simple Machine Learning Model

```python
python

from      sklearn.model_selection      import
train_test_split
from          sklearn.ensemble          import
RandomForestClassifier

# Split data
X_train,    X_test,    y_train,    y_test    =
train_test_split(df.drop('Purchased',   axis=1),
df['Purchased'], test_size=0.2)

# Train model
model = RandomForestClassifier(n_estimators=100)
model.fit(X_train, y_train)
```

Step 3: Deploying the Model as a Web Service

1. Convert Model to Azure ML Format

```python
python

import joblib
from azureml.core.model import Model

joblib.dump(model, "model.pkl")
```

```python
# Register model
Model.register(ws,       model_path="model.pkl",
model_name="recommendation-model")
```

2. **Deploy as an API Endpoint**

```python
python

from       azureml.core.webservice       import
AciWebservice, Webservice

deployment_config                         =
AciWebservice.deploy_configuration(cpu_cores=1,
memory_gb=1)
service  =  Model.deploy(ws,  "recommendation-
service", [model], deployment_config)
service.wait_for_deployment(show_output=True)
```

✓ Model is now **accessible via REST API**.
✓ Frontend applications can call the API to **recommend products**.

Real-World Example: Creating a Recommendation Engine for an Online Store

Scenario

An **e-commerce company** wants to improve **customer experience** by suggesting personalized products based on past purchases.

Solution Using Azure Machine Learning

1. **Collect User Data**
   - Extract purchase history from the **Azure SQL Database**.
   - Store it in **Azure Data Lake** for analysis.
2. **Train the Recommendation Model**
   - Use **Azure Machine Learning** with **Random Forest** or **Deep Learning (TensorFlow/PyTorch)**.
3. **Deploy the Model as an API**
   - Deploy on **Azure Kubernetes Service (AKS)** or **Azure Container Instances (ACI)**.
4. **Integrate into the E-Commerce Platform**
   - The **website calls the API** to **suggest products** dynamically.

Outcome

🖋 **Increased Conversions** – Customers see **personalized recommendations**.

📈 **Improved User Engagement** – Reduces bounce rates with targeted content.

💰 **Higher Revenue** – Users are **more likely to purchase recommended items**.

Conclusion

Azure provides **powerful AI and ML tools** to **build and deploy intelligent applications**.

✓ **Azure Machine Learning** – Best for **custom model training & deployment**.
✓ **Cognitive Services** – Provides **ready-to-use AI APIs** for vision, speech, and NLP.
✓ **Bot Services** – Enables **intelligent chatbot development**.

The **real-world example** demonstrated how an **e-commerce company built a recommendation engine** using **Azure Machine Learning** to improve customer experience and sales.

By mastering **Azure's AI capabilities**, businesses can **automate decisions, enhance customer interactions, and unlock new possibilities with data-driven insights**.

Key Takeaways

1. Azure ML helps train and deploy AI models at scale.
2. Cognitive Services provides pre-built AI models for quick integration.
3. Azure Bot Services enables chatbot development for automation.
4. Real-World Impact: An e-commerce platform increased sales with an AI-driven recommendation engine.

CHAPTER 18

IoT Solutions – Connecting Devices with Azure IoT Hub and Edge

Introduction

The **Internet of Things (IoT)** is transforming industries by connecting physical devices to the cloud, enabling **real-time data collection, automation, and predictive analytics.** From **smart home automation** to **industrial monitoring**, IoT solutions provide valuable insights that drive efficiency and innovation.

Azure offers a **comprehensive suite of IoT services** designed to manage, monitor, and secure **billions of connected devices.** The key services include:

- **Azure IoT Hub** – A central messaging hub for IoT device communication.
- **Azure IoT Central** – A managed IoT application platform for rapid deployment.
- **Azure IoT Edge** – Brings cloud intelligence to **edge devices** for real-time processing.

In this chapter, we will explore **Azure IoT services, device management, and security best practices.** We will also walk through a **real-world example of deploying an IoT solution for smart home automation with real-time data processing.**

Overview of Azure's IoT Services

1. Azure IoT Hub (Device Communication & Management)

Azure IoT Hub is a fully managed service that acts as a **message broker** between IoT devices and cloud applications.

Key Features:

✅ **Bi-Directional Communication** – Devices can **send telemetry** and **receive commands**.

✅ **Device Authentication** – Secure **per-device authentication** using X.509 certificates.

✅ **Scalability** – Supports **millions of devices** with high throughput.

✅ **Integration with AI & Analytics** – Connects with **Azure Machine Learning & Synapse Analytics** for real-time insights.

Use Cases:

- **Smart Home Automation** – Control and monitor home appliances remotely.
- **Industrial IoT (IIoT)** – Predictive maintenance in **manufacturing plants**.
- **Fleet Tracking** – Monitor vehicle status and optimize routes.

---

2. Azure IoT Central (No-Code IoT Platform)

Azure IoT Central is a **fully managed, low-code IoT solution** that simplifies device onboarding and management.

Key Features:

✅ **Pre-Built IoT Templates** – Quickly deploy solutions for **healthcare, retail, energy, and smart buildings**.
✅ **Dashboard & Insights** – Visualize real-time IoT data **without** **coding**.
✅ **Managed Security** – Built-in **data encryption and compliance**.

Use Cases:

- **Retail Inventory Tracking** – Monitor stock levels with **smart sensors**.
- **Smart Agriculture** – Optimize irrigation using **real-time soil moisture data**.
- **Cold Chain Logistics** – Ensure temperature compliance in **vaccine transportation**.

---

3. Azure IoT Edge (Bringing Cloud Intelligence to Devices)

Azure IoT Edge extends cloud capabilities to **edge devices**, allowing **real-time data processing** closer to where data is generated.

Key Features:

✅ **Run AI Models on Edge Devices** – Process data **locally** to reduce latency.

✅ **Offline Processing** – Continue operations even **without internet connectivity**.

✅ **Lower Cloud Costs** – Process data **on-premises** and send only relevant data to the cloud.

Use Cases:

- **Smart Traffic Management** – Analyze **vehicle congestion in real-time**.
- **Remote Oil & Gas Monitoring** – Detect leaks **without cloud dependency**.
- **AI-Driven Surveillance Cameras** – Perform **object detection on the edge**.

Managing and Securing IoT Devices

IoT deployments introduce **security challenges** as billions of devices connect to the internet. Proper **device management and security policies** are critical to prevent cyberattacks.

1. Best Practices for IoT Security

✓ **Per-Device Authentication** – Use **certificates and SAS tokens** for device identity.

✓ **End-to-End Encryption** – Encrypt **data in transit and at rest**.

✓ **Zero Trust Model** – Restrict access based on **device roles and policies**.

✓ **Regular Firmware Updates** – Patch vulnerabilities **remotely**.

✓ **Device Monitoring** – Detect anomalies using **Azure Security Center for IoT**.

---

2. Registering and Managing Devices in IoT Hub

Register a Device in IoT Hub (Using Azure CLI)

bash

```
az   iot   hub   create   --resource-group
MyResourceGroup --name MyIoTHub --sku S1
```

✓ Creates an **IoT Hub** with **secure messaging**.

Add a Device to IoT Hub

bash

```
az iot hub device-identity create --hub-name
MyIoTHub --device-id MySmartDevice
```

✓ Registers a **smart home device** in IoT Hub.

Monitor Telemetry from Devices

bash

```
az iot hub monitor-events --hub-name MyIoTHub --
output table
```

✔ Streams **real-time device data** from sensors.

Real-World Example: Deploying a Smart Home Automation IoT Solution

Scenario

A **home automation company** wants to develop a **smart thermostat** that automatically adjusts temperature based on weather conditions and user preferences.

Solution Using Azure IoT Services

1. **Smart Thermostat Devices** – Each thermostat has built-in **temperature sensors** and **Wi-Fi connectivity**.
2. **Azure IoT Hub** – Collects real-time **temperature data** and sends commands.
3. **Azure IoT Edge** – Runs **AI models on the thermostat** for **local decision-making**.

4. **Azure Functions** – Processes incoming data and triggers notifications.
5. **Power BI Dashboard** – Displays **real-time temperature insights** for homeowners.

Step 1: Deploy IoT Devices with Azure IoT Hub

Python Script to Simulate IoT Device Sending Data to IoT Hub

python

```python
import random
import time
from azure.iot.device import IoTHubDeviceClient,
Message

# Connect to Azure IoT Hub
CONNECTION_STRING                           =
"YOUR_IOT_HUB_DEVICE_CONNECTION_STRING"
client                                      =
IoTHubDeviceClient.create_from_connection_strin
g(CONNECTION_STRING)

# Simulate temperature sensor data
while True:
```

```
    temperature = round(random.uniform(18, 30),
2)

    message    =    Message(f'{{"temperature":
{temperature}}}')


    print(f"Sending message: {message}")
    client.send_message(message)
    time.sleep(5)  # Send data every 5 seconds
```

✓ **Simulates temperature readings** sent from a **smart thermostat** to IoT Hub.

Step 2: Deploy an AI Model on IoT Edge for Local Decision Making

Smart thermostats can **adjust temperature locally** using **Azure IoT Edge**.

bash

```
az   iot   edge   set-modules   --device-id
MySmartThermostat --hub-name MyIoTHub --content
./deployment.json
```

✓ Deploys a **machine learning model** on the **thermostat** to adjust temperature without **cloud dependency**.

Step 3: Process Data and Send Alerts Using Azure Functions

When **temperature exceeds 28°C**, Azure Functions sends **an alert to the user.**

python

```
import azure.functions as func
import json

def main(event: func.EventHubEvent):
    data                                    =
json.loads(event.get_body().decode('utf-8'))
    temperature = data.get("temperature")

    if temperature > 28:
        print(f"ALERT:      High      temperature
detected: {temperature}°C")
```

✓ **Triggers an alert when temperature crosses a threshold.**

Step 4: Visualize Smart Home Data in Power BI

Use **Azure Stream Analytics** to **push live sensor data** into **Power BI dashboards**.

sql

```
SELECT
    temperature,
    system.timestamp AS timestamp
INTO PowerBIOutput
FROM IoTHubInput
```

✓ Displays **real-time temperature data** in **interactive dashboards**.

Outcome

🏠 **Automated Home Temperature Control** – AI models optimize thermostat settings.

📈 **Real-Time Monitoring** – Homeowners **track temperature insights via Power BI**.

🔒 **Secure Device Communication** – IoT Hub ensures **end-to-end encryption**.

🏃 **Reduced Cloud Dependency** – IoT Edge **runs AI locally for instant decisions**.

Conclusion

Azure provides **powerful IoT services** that enable **secure, scalable, and intelligent** device management.

✓ **Azure IoT Hub** – Best for **device communication & management.**

✓ **Azure IoT Central** – Simplifies **IoT solution deployment.**

✓ **Azure IoT Edge** – Enables **real-time AI at the edge.**

The **real-world example** demonstrated how a **smart home automation system** can use **Azure IoT Hub, IoT Edge, and AI models** to create an intelligent **thermostat solution.**

By mastering **Azure IoT services,** businesses can **deploy smart, connected solutions** that **optimize operations and enhance customer experiences.**

Key Takeaways

1. **IoT Hub enables secure, bi-directional communication with devices.**

2. **IoT Edge allows real-time AI decision-making without cloud dependence.**

3. **IoT security best practices protect connected devices.**

4. **Real-World Impact** – A **smart home thermostat** optimized energy usage and **improved user experience.**

PART IV

GOVERNANCE, INTEGRATION, AND ADVANCED DEPLOYMENT

CHAPTER 19

Building Hybrid Cloud Solutions with Azure

Introduction

Many organizations operate in a **hybrid cloud environment**, where they combine **on-premises infrastructure** with **cloud resources** to achieve **scalability, flexibility, and security**. A hybrid cloud strategy allows businesses to **modernize their IT infrastructure** while still leveraging existing **on-premises investments**.

Microsoft **Azure offers a suite of hybrid cloud solutions**, including **Azure Stack, hybrid networking**, and **data synchronization services**, to help organizations seamlessly extend their on-premises environments to the cloud.

In this chapter, we will explore **Azure's hybrid cloud capabilities**, including **Azure Stack, hybrid networking, and data synchronization**. We will also walk through a **real-world example of extending an on-premises data center to the cloud using Azure Stack.**

Why Hybrid Cloud?

A hybrid cloud solution provides **the best of both worlds—** allowing organizations to keep **sensitive workloads on-premises** while leveraging the **scalability and agility of the cloud.**

Key Benefits of Hybrid Cloud

✓ **Scalability** – Expand computing and storage capacity on demand.

✓ **Cost Optimization** – Maintain **on-premises infrastructure** while using **cloud resources** as needed.

✓ **Regulatory Compliance** – Store sensitive data **locally** while still using **cloud computing power.**

✓ **Business Continuity** – Ensure **disaster recovery** and **high availability** with cloud-based backup solutions.

Azure Hybrid Cloud Solutions

1. Azure Stack: Extending Azure to On-Premises

Azure Stack is a **hybrid cloud platform** that brings **Azure services to on-premises environments**, allowing businesses to run cloud-based applications in **their own data centers.**

Key Features:

✓ **Run Azure Services Locally** – Deploy **VMs, Kubernetes, and AI models** on-premises.
✓ **Consistent Cloud & On-Prem Experience** – Unified **management & security policies.**
✓ **Disconnected Mode** – Run **Azure applications even without an internet connection.**

Use Cases:

- **Government & Finance** – Data residency requirements mandate **on-prem data storage.**
- **Retail & Manufacturing** – **Low-latency processing** for smart factories.
- **Healthcare** – Hospitals use Azure Stack for **patient data compliance.**

How Azure Stack Works

Azure Stack provides a **self-contained Azure environment** inside an organization's **data center**.

- **Azure Stack Hub** – Full-scale hybrid cloud for **enterprise workloads**.
- **Azure Stack Edge** – Optimized for **AI and IoT processing** at the edge.
- **Azure Stack HCI** – Hyperconverged infrastructure for **VM workloads**.

---

2. Hybrid Networking: Connecting On-Premises to Azure

A **hybrid network** ensures **secure, low-latency** communication between **on-prem data centers** and **Azure resources**.

Key Networking Services

Service	Description	Best Use Case
VPN Gateway	Creates **a secure tunnel** between on-premises and Azure.	Small/medium businesses needing secure connectivity.
Azure ExpressRoute	Provides a **private, high-speed** connection between Azure and on-prem.	Large enterprises needing **low-latency performance**.
Virtual WAN	Unifies branch office connectivity.	Multi-site organizations needing a global network.

Example: **Creating a VPN Connection to Azure**

```bash
az network vpn-connection create --resource-group MyResourceGroup --name MyVPN --vnet-name MyVNet --local-gateway-name MyOnPremGateway
```

✓ **Securely connects an on-prem network to Azure over VPN.**

3. Data Synchronization Between On-Prem and Azure

Hybrid cloud strategies often require **real-time data synchronization** between **on-premises databases** and **Azure cloud storage**.

Key Azure Data Sync Services

Service	Description	Use Case
Azure SQL Data Sync	Syncs data between **on-prem SQL databases** and **Azure SQL**.	Multi-location enterprises needing **real-time database replication**.
Azure Data Factory	Moves data from **on-prem systems** to Azure for analysis.	ETL pipelines for **big data analytics**.
Azure File Sync	Syncs **on-prem file servers** with **Azure Storage**.	File sharing across **multiple branch offices**.

Example: **Syncing an On-Prem SQL Database with Azure SQL**

sql

```
EXEC     sp_addsyncgroup     @sync_group    =
'OnPremToAzureSync'
```

✓ **Replicates on-prem SQL data to the cloud in real-time.**

Real-World Example: Extending an On-Premises Data Center to Azure with Azure Stack

Scenario

A **financial institution** wants to modernize its IT infrastructure **without moving all its data to the cloud** due to **regulatory constraints**.

Solution: Deploying a Hybrid Cloud Using Azure Stack

Step 1: Deploy Azure Stack in the Data Center

1. **Purchase Azure Stack hardware** from a certified vendor (**Dell, Lenovo, or HPE**).
2. **Install Azure Stack Hub** in the on-premises data center.

3. **Configure Identity and Access Management (IAM)** for **secure authentication**.

Step 2: Establish a Secure Network Connection to Azure

1. **Use ExpressRoute** to establish a **low-latency, private connection** between on-premises and Azure.
2. **Extend Virtual Networks** between **on-prem** and **Azure VMs**.
3. **Set Up Azure Firewall** for **advanced security**.

Step 3: Enable Data Synchronization

1. **Sync customer transactions between Azure SQL and on-prem SQL**.
2. **Enable Azure File Sync** to replicate **important financial records** across locations.
3. **Implement Backup & Disaster Recovery** using **Azure Backup**.

Outcome

✅ **Compliance & Security** – **Customer data remains on-prem** to meet regulations.
✅ **Scalability & Resilience** – The **financial system scales dynamically** using Azure resources.
✅ **Cost Efficiency** – **Hybrid cloud model** reduces the need for **expensive data center expansions**.

Conclusion

A **hybrid cloud approach** allows businesses to **extend their on-premises IT infrastructure** to Azure **without completely migrating to the cloud**.

✓ **Azure Stack** brings Azure services **to local data centers**.
✓ **Hybrid networking (VPN, ExpressRoute, Virtual WAN)** ensures **secure, seamless connectivity**.
✓ **Azure Data Sync solutions** enable **real-time data replication** between on-prem and cloud.

The **real-world example** demonstrated how a **financial institution** successfully extended its **on-premises infrastructure to Azure** using **Azure Stack, hybrid networking, and data synchronization**.

By **leveraging hybrid cloud solutions**, businesses can **modernize IT operations, reduce costs, and maintain security & compliance**.

Key Takeaways

1. **Hybrid cloud integrates on-prem and cloud environments** for **scalability and security**.
2. **Azure Stack enables on-premises cloud computing** while maintaining compliance.
3. **Hybrid networking (VPN, ExpressRoute) provides seamless connectivity** between Azure and data centers.
4. **Real-World Impact** – A **financial institution** extended its data center to Azure while **complying with data residency laws**.

CHAPTER 20

Integrating Third-Party Tools and Services with Azure

Introduction

Microsoft Azure is a powerful cloud platform, but **many businesses rely on third-party tools** to extend functionality, enhance automation, and integrate seamlessly with existing systems. Whether it's **third-party CRMs, API management tools, or multi-cloud strategies**, Azure provides flexible integration options to **maximize productivity and streamline business operations**.

In this chapter, we will explore how **Azure integrates with third-party solutions** using the **Azure Marketplace, API Management, and cross-cloud integrations**. We'll also walk through a **real-world example of a marketing firm integrating a third-party CRM with Azure** to improve customer engagement.

Extending Azure with Third-Party Solutions

1. Azure Marketplace: One-Click Third-Party Integrations

The **Azure Marketplace** is a digital store that offers **third-party applications, tools, and services** that can be deployed **directly into an Azure environment**.

Key Features:

✅ **Pre-Configured Solutions** – Deploy software like **Datadog, Splunk, Jenkins, and Palo Alto firewalls** instantly.

✅ **Pay-As-You-Go Pricing** – Integrated **billing within Azure** (no extra vendor contracts).

✅ **Security & Compliance** – Third-party solutions vetted for **enterprise security standards**.

Popular Third-Party Marketplace Solutions

Solution	Category	Use Case
Datadog	Monitoring & Logging	Application performance tracking.

Solution	Category	Use Case
Splunk	Security SIEM	& Centralized security monitoring.
Palo Alto NGFW	Firewall Security	& Advanced threat protection.
Jenkins	DevOps Automation	CI/CD pipeline automation.
WordPress on Azure	Web Hosting	Deploying a content management system (CMS).

Example: Deploying a Third-Party Firewall in Azure

To deploy **Palo Alto Next-Generation Firewall (NGFW)** for **cloud security**:

1. **Go to the Azure Marketplace** and search for **"Palo Alto Firewall"**.
2. Click **Create** → Choose **VM Size** → Configure **Networking & Security Settings**.
3. Deploy the firewall **to protect Azure workloads** from cyber threats.

✓ **Provides real-time network security** against attacks.

✓ **Integrates with Azure Security Center** for unified monitoring.

---

2. API Management: Connecting Third-Party Services

APIs enable businesses to **integrate third-party services** and build **scalable, connected applications**.

Azure API Management (APIM) acts as a **centralized gateway** for **securing, monitoring, and managing APIs**, whether they are hosted on **Azure, AWS, Google Cloud, or on-premises**.

Key Features:

✓ **API Gateway** – Securely expose internal services to external   users.

✓ **Traffic Management** – Control API rate limits & throttling.

✓ **Multi-Cloud & Hybrid Connectivity** – Connect APIs from **different clouds & on-prem environments**.

Example: Integrating a Third-Party Payment API with Azure Functions

Let's say an **e-commerce company** wants to **integrate Stripe's payment API** with **Azure Functions**.

Step 1: Deploy Azure API Management

```bash
az apim create --resource-group MyResourceGroup
--name MyAPIService --sku-name Consumption
```

✓ Creates an **Azure API Gateway** to manage external APIs.

Step 2: Securely Connect to Stripe API in Azure Functions

```python
import requests

STRIPE_API_URL                            =
"https://api.stripe.com/v1/charges"
HEADERS    =    {"Authorization":    "Bearer
sk_test_YourSecretKey"}

def create_charge(amount, currency):
```

```
data = {"amount": amount, "currency":
currency, "source": "tok_visa"}
    response = requests.post(STRIPE_API_URL,
headers=HEADERS, data=data)
    return response.json()
```

✓ **Processes payments** by integrating Stripe with **Azure Functions**.

Step 3: Monitor API Usage with APIM Analytics

- **View API requests, latency, and failure rates** in the **Azure API Management dashboard**.

---

3. Multi-Cloud and Cross-Platform Integrations

Many enterprises use **multiple cloud providers** (Azure, AWS, Google Cloud) to **avoid vendor lock-in**. Azure provides **native integrations** with **AWS, Google Cloud, and SaaS applications**.

Key Multi-Cloud Integration Tools

Azure Service	Integrates With	Purpose
Azure Arc	On-Prem & Multi-Cloud	Manage VMs, Kubernetes across clouds.
Azure Logic Apps	Salesforce, Slack, Google Drive	Automate workflows across platforms.
Azure Data Factory	AWS S3, Google BigQuery	Move & process data between clouds.
Azure DevOps	GitHub, Jenkins, AWS CodePipeline	CI/CD automation across environments.

Example: Connecting Azure and AWS for Hybrid Cloud

A **media company** needs to **store videos on AWS S3** while using **Azure AI for video processing**.

Step 1: Connect Azure and AWS S3 using Data Factory

bash

```
az datafactory create --name MyDataFactory --resource-group MyResourceGroup
```

✓ Sets up **Azure Data Factory** for **cross-cloud data transfer**.

Step 2: Copy Data from AWS S3 to Azure Storage

json

```json
{
    "type": "CopyActivity",
    "inputs": [{"name": "AWS-S3-Video-Files"}],
    "outputs": [{"name": "Azure-Blob-Storage"}]
}
```

✓ Automates **data movement between AWS and Azure**.

Real-World Example: Integrating a Third-Party CRM with Azure for Customer Engagement

Scenario

A **marketing firm** wants to integrate **Salesforce CRM** with Azure to **streamline customer engagement** and gain **real-time insights**.

Solution: Connecting Salesforce CRM to Azure Services

1. **Use Azure Logic Apps** to connect Salesforce with Azure SQL.
2. **Send Customer Data to Power BI** for **real-time analytics**.
3. **Enable Automated Email Campaigns** using **Azure Functions & SendGrid**.

Step 1: Automate Customer Data Sync Using Logic Apps

1. **Go to Azure Portal** → Create **Logic App**.
2. Add **Salesforce Connector** → Fetch new leads every 10 minutes.
3. **Store lead data** in **Azure SQL Database**.

sql

```
INSERT INTO Leads (Name, Email, LeadSource)
VALUES ('John Doe', 'johndoe@email.com', 'Web
Form');
```

✓ **Automatically syncs customer data** from Salesforce to Azure.

Step 2: Visualize Customer Data in Power BI

Use **Azure Synapse Analytics** to analyze **customer trends**.

- **View lead conversion rates.**
- **Segment users based on behavior.**

sql

```sql
SELECT LeadSource, COUNT(*) AS TotalLeads
FROM Leads
GROUP BY LeadSource;
```

✓ **Generates real-time insights** on customer behavior.

Step 3: Automate Marketing Emails with Azure Functions

python

```python
import sendgrid
```

```
from sendgrid.helpers.mail import Mail

def send_email(to_email, subject, content):
    sg                                      =
sendgrid.SendGridAPIClient(api_key="YOUR_SENDGR
ID_API_KEY")
    mail                                    =
Mail(from_email="marketing@company.com",
to_emails=to_email,              subject=subject,
plain_text_content=content)
    sg.send(mail)
```

✓ **Automatically sends follow-up emails to new leads.**

Outcome

📈 **Real-Time Customer Insights** – Marketing teams track lead conversion rates **instantly**.

🎯 **Automated Engagement** – Personalized emails **increase conversions**.

🚀 **Seamless Integration** – Salesforce CRM syncs **directly with Azure SQL & Power BI**.

Conclusion

Azure provides **multiple ways** to integrate **third-party tools and cloud services**, enabling businesses to build **scalable, connected solutions**.

✓ **Azure Marketplace** – Deploy **third-party applications** with **one** **click**.
✓ **Azure API Management** – Securely integrate **external APIs**.
✓ **Multi-Cloud Integrations** – Use **Azure with AWS, Google Cloud, and SaaS tools**.

The **real-world example** demonstrated how a **marketing firm used Salesforce, Power BI, and Azure Functions** to **automate customer engagement and gain actionable insights**.

By **leveraging third-party integrations**, businesses can **enhance productivity, streamline operations, and maximize cloud capabilities**.

Key Takeaways

1. **Azure Marketplace simplifies third-party deployments.**
2. **API Management enables secure external service integration.**
3. **Multi-cloud tools (Azure Arc, Data Factory) allow cross-cloud data management.**
4. **Real-World Impact** – A **marketing firm automated lead tracking & engagement** using **Azure & Salesforce CRM.**

CHAPTER 21

Azure for DevOps and Continuous Delivery

Introduction

DevOps is a **combination of software development (Dev) and IT operations (Ops)** that aims to automate the **software development lifecycle (SDLC)** to improve **collaboration, speed, and reliability**.

Azure DevOps provides a **complete suite of DevOps tools** that help organizations **build, test, and deploy applications faster and with greater efficiency**. By leveraging **Continuous Integration (CI) and Continuous Delivery (CD)** pipelines, businesses can **automate builds, run tests, and deploy code seamlessly**.

In this chapter, we'll explore how **Azure DevOps, CI/CD pipelines, and release management** work. We will also walk through a **real-world example of setting up a CI/CD pipeline for a web application** that speeds up releases and improves reliability.

What is Azure DevOps?

Azure DevOps is a **cloud-based DevOps platform** that provides tools for **collaboration, automation, and monitoring** throughout the software development lifecycle.

Key Features of Azure DevOps

Feature	Description
Azure Repos	Git repositories for version control.
Azure Pipelines	CI/CD automation for builds, tests, and deployments.
Azure Test Plans	Automated and manual testing for quality assurance.
Azure Artifacts	Package management for dependencies (NuGet, npm, Maven).
Azure Boards	Agile project management with Kanban boards and issue tracking.

1. What is Continuous Integration (CI)?

CI is the **practice of frequently integrating code changes** into a shared repository. Each integration **triggers an automated build and test process** to catch issues early.

✓ **Detects bugs faster**

✓ **Reduces integration conflicts**

✓ **Ensures code is always deployable**

---

2. What is Continuous Delivery (CD)?

CD automates **deployments to staging and production environments** after successful CI builds.

✓ **Enables fast, frequent releases**

✓ **Reduces manual intervention**

✓ **Improves software reliability**

---

3. Key Components of a CI/CD Pipeline

A complete **CI/CD pipeline** includes:

1 **Source Code Management** – Store code in **Azure Repos (GitHub, Bitbucket, or GitLab also supported)**.

2 **Build Pipeline** – Automate builds with **Azure Pipelines**.

3 **Automated Testing** – Run unit and integration tests before deployment.

4 **Release Management** – Deploy applications to **staging and production environments**.

5 **Monitoring & Feedback** – Use **Azure Monitor and Application Insights** to track performance.

Setting Up a CI/CD Pipeline in Azure DevOps

Step 1: Create a Git Repository in Azure Repos

1. **Go to Azure DevOps** → Select **Azure Repos**.
2. Click **Create a new repository** → Choose **Git**.
3. Clone the repository locally:

```bash
git clone https://dev.azure.com/your-org/your-repo.git
```

Step 2: Define a Build Pipeline (CI)

1. **Go to Azure Pipelines** → Click **New Pipeline**.
2. Choose **YAML Pipeline** and define the build process:

```yaml
yaml

trigger:
- main

pool:
  vmImage: 'ubuntu-latest'

steps:
- task: UseNode@1
  inputs:
    version: '14.x'

- script: npm install
  displayName: 'Install Dependencies'

- script: npm test
  displayName: 'Run Tests'

- script: npm run build
  displayName: 'Build Application'
```

✓ This pipeline **installs dependencies, runs tests, and builds the app** when changes are pushed to the main branch.

Step 3: Add Automated Tests

Example: Running Unit Tests in Python

yaml

```
- script: pytest tests/
  displayName: 'Run Unit Tests'
```

✓ Ensures **code quality** before deployment.

Step 4: Deploy to Azure Web App (CD)

1. **Define Deployment Stage in the YAML file**:

yaml

```
- task: AzureWebApp@1
  inputs:
    azureSubscription: 'MyAzureSubscription'
    appName: 'my-web-app'
    package:
'$(System.DefaultWorkingDirectory)/dist'
```

✓ This deploys the web application **to Azure App Service**.

Step 5: Configure Release Management

1. **Go to Azure DevOps** → Select **Releases**.
2. Click **New Release Pipeline** → Choose **Azure App Service Deployment**.
3. Select **the artifact from the CI build**.
4. Add **Approval Gates** (manual or automated approval).
5. Click **Create & Deploy**.

✓ Ensures **controlled, reliable deployments**.

Real-World Example: End-to-End CI/CD Pipeline for a Web Application

Scenario

A **software company** is building a **React-based web application**. They want to:

- **Automate testing and deployment** after each code change.
- **Reduce deployment failures** by validating code before releases.

- **Deploy updates seamlessly** without downtime.

Solution: Setting Up a Full CI/CD Pipeline in Azure DevOps

1. Source Control: Developers push code to **Azure Repos Git**.

2. CI Pipeline: Azure Pipelines **runs tests and builds the app** automatically.

3. CD Pipeline: Deployments are pushed to **Azure App Service** for production.

4. Monitoring & Feedback: **Azure Monitor** provides **real-time logs & performance metrics**.

Step 1: Create a React App and Push to Azure Repos

bash

```
npx create-react-app my-app
cd my-app
git init
git add .
```

```
git commit -m "Initial Commit"
git push origin main
```

✓ The **CI pipeline is triggered** when code is pushed.

Step 2: Define Build and Test Steps

Modify the `azure-pipelines.yml` file:

```yaml
yaml

trigger:
- main

pool:
  vmImage: 'ubuntu-latest'

steps:
- task: NodeTool@0
  inputs:
    versionSpec: '14.x'

- script: npm install
  displayName: 'Install Dependencies'

- script: npm test
  displayName: 'Run Tests'
```

```
- script: npm run build
  displayName: 'Build React App'
```

✓ Runs **unit tests and builds the React app**.

Step 3: Deploy to Azure App Service

Add CD pipeline to deploy the React app:

yaml

```
- task: AzureWebApp@1
  inputs:
    azureSubscription: 'Azure-Subscription'
    appName: 'my-react-app'
    package:
'$(System.DefaultWorkingDirectory)/build'
```

✓ Deploys **to production automatically**.

Outcome

🚀 **Deployment Speed** – New features are **deployed in minutes**, not days.

🔍 **Improved Reliability** – Bugs are **caught early** with **automated** **testing**.

📊 **Monitoring & Feedback** – **Application Insights** tracks **performance & errors**.

Conclusion

Azure DevOps **empowers development teams** to build, test, and deploy applications faster.

✓ **CI/CD Pipelines** automate **testing and deployment**.

✓ **Azure Pipelines** enables **secure, scalable CI/CD workflows**.

✓ **Release Management** ensures **controlled, rollback-friendly deployments**.

The **real-world example** demonstrated how a **React web application** was deployed **end-to-end using Azure DevOps**, leading to **faster releases and fewer failures**.

By mastering **CI/CD in Azure**, teams can **deliver high-quality software at speed and scale**.

Key Takeaways

1. **CI/CD in Azure automates software delivery** for faster releases.

2. **Azure DevOps provides tools for repo management, testing, and deployment.**

3. **Automated testing reduces bugs and improves reliability.**

4. **Real-World Impact** – A **React app was deployed end-to-end** with Azure Pipelines, **speeding up releases & improving quality.**

CHAPTER 22

Future Trends in Azure and Cloud Computing

Introduction

Cloud computing is evolving at an **unprecedented pace**, transforming **how businesses, governments, and individuals** use technology. As organizations demand **more speed, scalability, and intelligence**, Azure continues to **lead the innovation frontier** by integrating **edge computing, AI-driven automation, serverless advancements, and sustainability initiatives**.

In this chapter, we will explore the **emerging trends shaping the future of Azure and cloud computing**, including **edge computing, AI integration, the evolution of serverless, and sustainability efforts**. Finally, we'll look at a **real-world example of a futuristic smart city leveraging Azure to optimize energy use and connectivity**.

1. Edge Computing: Bringing Cloud Capabilities Closer to Users

What is Edge Computing?

Edge computing shifts **computing power closer to the source of data**, reducing **latency, bandwidth costs, and reliance on centralized cloud data centers**. Rather than **processing data in Azure's core cloud**, **edge devices** analyze information **locally** before sending relevant insights to the cloud.

Why is Edge Computing the Future?

✓ **Ultra-Low Latency** – Devices process data **in milliseconds**, ideal for **autonomous vehicles, IoT, and real-time analytics**.

✓ **Bandwidth Optimization** – Reduces **data transfer costs** by only sending important information to the cloud.

✓ **Resilience & Offline Processing** – Operates **even without an internet connection**, making it ideal for **remote industries like oil rigs or offshore wind farms**.

Azure's Edge Computing Offerings

Technology	Description	Use Case
Azure IoT Edge	Runs AI and analytics directly on edge devices.	Smart factories, retail automation, healthcare AI.
Azure Stack Edge	Cloud-managed hardware for **on-prem** **AI and analytics**.	Self-driving cars, security surveillance, real-time video processing.
Azure Arc	Manages **multi-cloud** and edge workloads from a single interface.	Hybrid cloud strategies, Kubernetes at the edge.

Example: Edge AI in a Retail Store

📌 A **retail chain** uses **Azure IoT Edge** to **process customer foot traffic, predict demand, and adjust in-store promotions in real time**—all **without needing an internet connection**.

2. Serverless Computing Evolution: Beyond Traditional Cloud Models

What is Serverless Computing?

Serverless computing allows developers to **run applications without managing servers**. Azure automatically **scales, optimizes, and charges only for execution time.**

How Serverless is Changing the Cloud?

✓ **Faster Development** – No need to provision or manage servers.

✓ **Cost-Efficient** – Pay only for **actual execution time**.

✓ **Infinite Scalability** – Automatically adapts **to demand spikes**.

Azure's Next-Generation Serverless Offerings

Service	Description	Use Case
Azure Functions	Event-driven serverless execution.	**Real-time data processing, chatbots, API automation.**

Service	Description	Use Case
Azure Logic Apps	Automates workflows between cloud services.	**Automated approvals, SaaS integrations**.
Azure Event Grid	Event-driven messaging between applications.	**IoT telemetry, financial transaction alerts**.

Example: Serverless Finance Automation

📌 A **FinTech company** uses **Azure Functions** to **automatically detect fraudulent transactions** by **analyzing payment behaviors in real time**.

3. AI & Cloud Integration: The Future of Smart Applications

How AI is Transforming Cloud Computing

Artificial Intelligence (AI) is **deeply embedded** into cloud services, allowing businesses to **build smarter applications** with **automated decision-making, predictive analytics, and natural language processing**.

Azure's AI-Powered Cloud Offerings

Technology	Description	Use Case
Azure OpenAI Service	Integrates GPT-powered AI into applications.	AI chatbots, automated content generation, coding assistants.
Azure Cognitive Services	Pre-trained AI models for vision, speech, and language.	Sentiment analysis, OCR, voice assistants.
Azure Synapse Analytics + AI	AI-powered data analytics platform.	Predictive maintenance, business intelligence dashboards.

Example: AI-Powered Manufacturing

✦ A **smart factory** integrates **Azure OpenAI** to analyze **machine performance logs**, predicting failures before they happen—**reducing downtime by 30%**.

4. Sustainable Cloud Computing: Green Innovation in Azure

The Environmental Impact of Cloud Computing

Data centers consume **massive energy**, contributing to **carbon emissions**. **Microsoft Azure** is leading the charge toward **sustainable, carbon-neutral cloud solutions**.

Azure's Sustainability Initiatives

✇ **Carbon-Neutral by 2030** – Microsoft pledges **100% renewable energy** for Azure.

✇ **Azure Sustainable Datacenters** – Water-cooled, solar-powered datacenters.

✇ **Emissions Monitoring** – **Azure Sustainability Calculator** tracks **carbon footprints**.

Example: Green Energy Optimization for Enterprises

📌 A **logistics company** uses **Azure AI** to optimize delivery routes, **reducing fuel consumption by 20%**, lowering both **costs and emissions**.

Real-World Example: Smart Cities Leveraging Azure for the Future

Scenario

A **futuristic smart city** integrates **Azure AI, IoT, and Edge** **computing** to **optimize energy use, reduce congestion,** **and enhance public safety**.

How Azure Powers the Smart City

1⬜ **Smart Energy Grid (Azure IoT Edge)** – AI-driven **power distribution** predicts energy demand **across** **neighborhoods**.

2⬜ **Traffic Optimization (Azure AI + Edge Computing)** – **AI-powered sensors adjust traffic lights** based on **real-time congestion data**.

3⬜ **Public Safety Monitoring (Azure Cognitive Services)** – **Real-time facial recognition** improves **security in public areas**.

4⬜ **Autonomous Public Transport (Azure Machine Learning)** – Self-driving buses **adapt routes dynamically**.

Outcome

🌐 **Reduced Carbon Footprint** – The city achieves a **30% energy efficiency boost**.

🚦 **Less Traffic Congestion** – Commute times **drop by 40%** with AI-powered traffic lights.

🛡 **Improved Public Safety** – Crime detection **improves with real-time AI analytics**.

Conclusion

Cloud computing is entering **a new era** driven by **edge computing, AI, serverless architectures, and sustainability**. **Azure continues to push boundaries**, helping businesses and cities become **smarter, faster, and greener**.

✓ **Edge Computing** reduces latency and enables real-time AI.

✓ **Serverless Computing** evolves to **eliminate infrastructure management**.

✓ **AI-Powered Cloud Services** transform **analytics, automation, and decision-making**.

✓ **Sustainability Initiatives** make Azure a leader in **eco-friendly cloud solutions**.

The **real-world smart city example** demonstrates how **Azure's cutting-edge innovations** optimize **energy use, connectivity, and public services**, setting the stage for **the future of digital transformation**.

By **staying ahead of these trends**, organizations can leverage **Azure's latest advancements to innovate, scale, and build a sustainable future**.

Key Takeaways

1. **Edge computing enhances real-time AI and IoT processing.**
2. **Serverless architectures simplify cloud automation and reduce costs.**
3. **AI-driven cloud solutions optimize business intelligence and automation.**
4. **Azure leads the future of green, carbon-neutral cloud computing.**

5. **Real-World Impact:** A **smart city integrates Azure AI, IoT, and Edge** to **enhance energy efficiency, traffic control, and public safety**.

CHAPTER 23

The Journey Ahead – Mastering Azure and Beyond

Introduction

Congratulations! You've embarked on a **transformative journey into Microsoft Azure**, gaining the knowledge and skills to **build, deploy, and manage cloud solutions with confidence**. But this is just the beginning.

Cloud computing is a rapidly evolving field, and **mastering Azure is not just about learning technology—it's about embracing a mindset of continuous learning and innovation**.

In this final chapter, we will:
✓ **Recap the core concepts covered in this book.**
✓ **Explore career opportunities in Azure and cloud computing.**
✓ **Highlight the importance of lifelong learning.**
✓ **Share real-world stories of professionals who**

advanced their careers by mastering Azure—inspiring you to keep exploring and innovating.

---

1. Recap of Azure Fundamentals

Let's summarize the **key topics** covered in this book to reinforce your understanding of Azure.

Core Azure Concepts You've Learned

Category	Key Topics Covered
Cloud Basics	Azure services, cloud computing models, regions & availability zones.
Compute	Virtual Machines (VMs), Azure Kubernetes Service (AKS), Serverless Functions.
Networking	Virtual Networks, ExpressRoute, VPN, Hybrid Cloud.
Storage & Data	Azure Blob Storage, SQL Database, Cosmos DB, Data Analytics.
Security & DevOps	Identity Management, Azure Security Center, CI/CD Pipelines.

Category	Key Topics Covered
Emerging Trends	AI, Machine Learning, Edge Computing, Sustainability.

With these skills, you now have the **foundational knowledge** to **build and optimize cloud solutions** in a professional setting.

---

2. Career Opportunities in Azure & Cloud Computing

Cloud computing is one of the **fastest-growing fields**, and **Azure expertise** is in high demand.

Top Career Paths in Azure

Role	Responsibilities	Average Salary (USD)
Cloud Engineer	Deploys and manages cloud infrastructure.	$100,000+

Role	Responsibilities	Average Salary (USD)
Azure Solutions Architect	Designs scalable Azure-based applications.	$140,000+
DevOps Engineer	Builds CI/CD pipelines and automates deployments.	$120,000+
Cloud Security Engineer	Ensures Azure environments are secure and compliant.	$130,000+
Data Engineer	Works with data pipelines and analytics on Azure.	$115,000+

✓ **Certifications like AZ-900, AZ-104, and AZ-305** can help advance your career.
✓ **Industries including healthcare, finance, retail, and tech rely on Azure skills.**
✓ **Freelancing and consulting opportunities** are growing in cloud computing.

◆ **Next Steps:** Build real-world projects, contribute to open-source cloud projects, and explore career paths aligned with your interests.

3. Lifelong Learning in Cloud Technologies

Technology evolves **constantly**, and **staying ahead** in the cloud industry requires **continuous learning**.

How to Stay Updated with Azure?

✓ **Microsoft Learn** – Free, interactive Azure training: https://learn.microsoft.com

✓ **Azure Certifications** – Advance your skills with **Microsoft Certified** paths.

✓ **Tech Communities & Forums** – Join **Azure Tech Groups, LinkedIn Cloud Communities, and Stack Overflow discussions**.

✓ **Experiment with New Azure Services** – Set up **Azure Free Tier** projects to practice real-world scenarios.

✓ **Follow Industry Leaders** – Stay updated with **Azure blogs, conferences (Ignite), and YouTube tutorials.**

✦ **Cloud professionals who continuously upskill remain competitive and future-proof their careers.**

4. Real-World Stories: How Mastering Azure Changed Careers

📖 Story 1: From IT Admin to Cloud Engineer

✦ **Background:** John worked as an **IT Administrator** for years but saw the demand shifting to cloud technologies.

✦ **Action:** He **learned Azure on Microsoft Learn**, completed an **AZ-104 certification**, and built small **cloud projects**.

✦ **Result:** He **transitioned into a Cloud Engineer role**, doubling his salary and working with **scalable cloud solutions**.

📖 Story 2: A Software Developer Automates Deployments with Azure DevOps

✦ **Background:** Maria, a **software developer**, wanted to automate **code deployments** and improve project efficiency.

✦ **Action:** She **built CI/CD pipelines** using **Azure DevOps** and integrated **Infrastructure as Code (IaC)** with Terraform.

◆ **Result:** Her company **reduced deployment times from 4 hours to 10 minutes**, and she was promoted to **DevOps Engineer**.

📖 Story 3: A Startup Adopting Azure AI for Growth

◆ **Background:** A startup in **healthcare AI** needed a **scalable cloud solution** to analyze patient data securely.

◆ **Action:** They implemented **Azure Machine Learning and Cognitive Services** to **automate medical diagnosis predictions**.

◆ **Result:** Their solution **reduced diagnosis time by 50%**, secured **funding from investors**, and expanded globally.

---

5. Your Next Steps: Continuing Your Azure Journey

Now that you have mastered **Azure fundamentals**, what's next?

Practical Ways to Apply Your Knowledge

✅ **Build a Cloud Portfolio** – Create projects showcasing real-world **Azure** **applications**.

✅ **Contribute to Open-Source** – Work on **Azure-based GitHub** **projects**.

✅ **Network with Professionals** – Join **Azure Meetups, LinkedIn Groups, and Microsoft Communities**.

✅ **Explore Advanced Certifications** – Consider **AZ-305 (Architect), AZ-400 (DevOps), or AI-102 (AI Engineer)**.

✅ **Apply for Cloud Roles** – Update your **resume with Azure experience**, apply for jobs, or offer **freelance cloud solutions**.

⬥ **Azure is constantly evolving—your learning never stops!**

Conclusion: The Future is Cloud, and You're Ready for It

Cloud computing is shaping the future of technology, and **Azure is at the center of this transformation.**

✔ **You've learned how to build, deploy, and scale solutions on Azure.**

✔ **You understand DevOps, security, AI, and emerging**

cloud   trends.
✓ You're equipped with skills to advance your career in cloud computing.

✹ Remember, the most successful cloud professionals are those who never stop learning. Keep building, keep experimenting, and keep innovating!

The **real-world success stories** shared in this chapter prove that **mastering Azure opens limitless career opportunities**. Your journey in Azure is just beginning— **the future is yours to shape.**

Final Takeaways: Mastering Azure and Beyond

✓ **Azure is a powerful platform** for compute, storage, AI, DevOps,   and   security.
✓ **Cloud careers are in high demand**, with roles in **engineering, security, AI, and DevOps.**
✓ **Continuous learning is key**—stay updated with **Microsoft Learn, certifications, and hands-on projects.**
✓ **Real-world projects and networking** accelerate career growth.

✓ The future of Azure includes AI, edge computing, sustainability, and hybrid cloud solutions.

🚀 The future is cloud—keep innovating, keep exploring, and master Azure! 🚀

End of Book: "Azure Fundamentals — Develop and Deploy Cloud Solutions with Confidence"

✹ Thank you for embarking on this journey! Your path to Azure mastery starts here. Now, go build something amazing!